Be Up and Doing

Lessons for Life

By
John M. Butler

Gaithersburg, Maryland

Dedication:

To my six children
(Amanda, Marshall, Katy, Emma, Ethan, and Bailey)
who inspire me with their desire
to learn, act, share and become
true disciples of Jesus Christ

This work is not an official publication of The Church of Jesus Christ of Latter-day Saints. The views expressed herein are the responsibility of the author and do not necessarily represent the position of the Church, the U.S. Department of Commerce, or the National Institute of Standards and Technology.

Butler, John M.
Be Up and Doing: Lessons for Life
ISBN: 9798748985673
    1. Spirituality
    2. Religion

Contents

Background on the Author 4

Introduction ...…..… 5

For Seminary Graduates and Teachers................................. 7

Chapter 1: Be Up and Doing: Setting and Achieving Goals with Vision.... 10

Chapter 2: Revelation: Activate Your Spiritual Smart Phone & Call Home. 18

Chapter 3: The Rod, the Path, and the Tree: Coming Unto Christ...…....... 35

Chapter 4: Prepare for Your Temple Blessings.......…...….................... 39

Chapter 5: The Kirtland Temple and the Gathering of Israel..…............ 50

Chapter 6: The Doctrine of Returning and Reporting. ….....…................ 63

Chapter 7: Learning in the Light of the Restoration.......................... 79

Chapter 8: Our Earthly Apprenticeship: Learning to Emulate Jesus Christ. 84

Chapter 9: Forming, Storming, Norming, and Performing................... 91

Chapter 10: The Book of Mormon and the Value of Scripture Study........ 100

Chapter 11: Keeping on the Covenant Path with Vigilance and Precision... 107

Chapter 12: Facing Closed Doors: Pressing Forward After Failures…....... 112

*Materials in this book were adapted from talks shared
in the Seneca Maryland Stake from 2016 to 2021
while the author served in the stake presidency*

Background on the Author

I was blessed to grow up in a family that loves and lives the teachings of the Restored Gospel of Jesus Christ. As such, I have made and strive to keep sacred covenants that bind me to our Father in Heaven and our Savior Jesus Christ. Some of my father's ancestors personally knew the Prophet Joseph Smith – and they suffered perilous persecution with other early Latter-day Saints. More recently, my mother also suffered persecution from her parents when she joined the Church. While I am a sixth generation member of the Church of Jesus Christ of Latter-day Saints, *I, like my mother, am a first generation convert.* I have come to know for myself through my scripture study and personal experiences that this is His Church and His Restored Gospel! I know that The Book of Mormon is Another Testament of Jesus Christ and stands alongside the Holy Bible in providing a witness to the world of our Savior Jesus Christ and of His love for us personally. I have studied its teachings and messages carefully and have found peace and joy and comfort since I first read The Book of Mormon from cover to cover as a 13-year-old boy.

The night before I was sustained and set-apart in a life-changing calling in the Church of Jesus Christ of Latter-day Saints, I read the following scripture in The Book of Mormon: "Thus God has provided a means that man, through faith, might work mighty miracles; therefore, *he becometh a great benefit to his fellow beings*" (Mosiah 8:18; emphasis added). These words have inspired me. I want to become a great benefit to my brothers and sisters on this earth through service and through sharing my testimony of the blessings of the Gospel of Jesus Christ. I desire to live up to the aspirations of the Thirteenth Article of Faith – in particular, "in doing good to all men [and women]."

Introduction

I prepared this book out of love for the wonderful youth of the Seneca Maryland Stake who I have had the privilege to work with for many years. They are amazing young women and young men bound for great things! These lessons for life have been adapted from talks given over the years in our stake, or in the case of the last chapter to students and faculty at BYU Idaho.

The title of this book "Be Up and Doing" comes from Alma 60:24 as part of a letter written by Captain Moroni, a Nephite military leader who lived in ancient America a few dozen years before Christ's birth. *To "be up and doing" is to take action in choosing the right.* In a scathing letter to a government leader thought to be shirking his duty in defending his country and people, Captain Moroni invites this leader – and by extension each of us – to "be up and doing." This book explores how we may accomplish this feat.

Captain Moroni is described by the prophet-editor Mormon as a "strong and mighty man" (Alma 48:11) and someone worthy of emulation (see Alma 48:17). Mormon is so impressed by Captain Moroni that he names his own son after this mighty leader who raised the title of liberty. After examining his nation's extensive historical and religious records, Mormon shares seven qualities or characteristics of Captain Moroni as "a man...": (1) "of perfect understanding", (2) "that did not delight in bloodshed", (3) "whose soul did joy in the liberty and freedom of his country", (4) "whose heart did swell with thanksgiving to his God", (5) "who did labor exceedingly for the welfare and safety of his people", (6) "who was firm in the faith of Christ", and (7) "like unto Ammon...and... the other sons of Mosiah...and also Alma and his sons, for they were all men of God" (Alma 48:11-13,18).

These are wonderful qualities. The phrase "a man" makes these qualities symbolic and applicable to all of us – *men and women* who seek to be disciples of Jesus Christ. Interestingly Mormon provides *seven* characteristics of Captain Moroni, much like John the Revelator uses *seven* churches in the Book of Revelation to represent a complete or perfect representation applicable to all of us.

We, like Captain Moroni, can develop these qualities of wisdom, peacefulness, patriotism, gratitude, hard work, rock-solid faith, and godliness through a lifetime of service. The Lord wishes to lay "the foundation of a great work" (D&C 64:33) in our lives as we give Him our "heart and a willing mind" (D&C 64:34). Truly from "small things," such as simple acts of service performed with love, will come "that which is great."

A few months before he received the Gold Plates in September 1827, young Joseph Smith was met on a road near the Hill Cumorah one evening and chastised by his angel tutor Moroni. According to his mother's record, Joseph was told by Moroni that he "had not been engaged enough in the work of the Lord; that the time had come for the record to be brought forth; and that [he, Joseph] must *be up and doing*, and set [himself] about the things which God had commanded [him] to do." (*History of Joseph Smith by His Mother*, p. 100, emphasis added). I find it interesting that a second Moroni used the same phrase "be up and doing" in encouraging faithfulness and greater diligence.

This book explores aspects of what it means to be up and doing as we seek to become true disciples of Jesus Christ. At the beginning of each chapter, a scripture and a few thoughts on important principles are shared in italics. It is hoped that applying these principles will be a blessing in your life.

For Seminary Graduates and Teachers

I grew up in the Maryville Branch located in the Liberty Missouri Stake. Our branch only had about 100 active members so we got to know each other fairly well. Brother Ron Eckerson faithfully and diligently taught me all four years of early morning seminary. I was the first four-year early morning seminary graduate in my branch. Our seminary class started at 6AM because we were all in marching band and had to be on the practice field at 7AM. Brother Eckerson was also my home teaching companion and my high school cross-country coach. He had a huge influence in the person I am today.

Perhaps sometimes you feel alone in your beliefs and efforts trying to live the high standards of the Gospel of Jesus Christ in what is sometimes a crazy and turbulent world. I know what that feels like. I was the *only* graduate in my seminary class thirty years ago. My senior year our seminary class consisted of five people: myself, my sister, my brother, and two kids from another family. Our class consisted of one senior (me), one junior, one sophomore, and two freshmen. Occasionally a less active member would show up for a lesson, but it was usually just the five of us. Be grateful to live in an area that has so many strong members of the Church – and wonderful seminary teachers and bishops.

Brother Eckerson shared more than 600 early morning gospel lessons with me. Some lessons were not the most exciting and I must admit that I probably fell asleep a time or two. My seminary teacher taught me by example the importance of perseverance as he kept going. His lessons exposed me to the writings of Hugh Nibley and the words of prophets ancient and modern. I have grown to love and appreciate these prophets and Church scholars in recent years through my own gospel study.

When we studied church history my senior year, I can recall studying the sacrifices of early Latter-day Saints and their efforts to live the law of consecration. As a high school student, I came to understand the Gospel of Jesus Christ because I saw it being lived firsthand in my seminary teacher's interactions with me. Looking back, I can see the love that Ron Eckerson had for me and his willingness to sacrifice sleep and time with his young family to prepare lessons that he delivered morning after morning after morning. My seminary teacher – and all seminary teachers – come closer to living the law of consecration in their service to you as their students as much as anyone in your life so far with possibly the exception of your bishop and your parents. I hope that you take the time to thank them for all they have done for you.

Seminary instilled in me a love for the scriptures. It prepared me for my full-time mission, which I started in Boston, Massachusetts, about a year after my seminary graduation.

Seminary began for me a life-long effort and journey to know and live the Gospel of Jesus Christ. I hope your seminary experience will do the same for you. The choice is yours with the course you will take for the rest of your mortal lives.

You have been exposed to the pages and teachings of the Book of Mormon. You have studied the words of our Savior. You have learned about men and women who knew Him and loved Him. I hope that in the early morning hours that you were awake in seminary you have gained a love and appreciation for our Savior Jesus Christ and His atoning sacrifice for you. This is why we have the seminary program in The Church of Jesus Christ of Latter-day Saints – so that you can come to know and love our Savior.

May your seminary experience be but the beginning of diligent personal scripture study. I have read thousands of books in my life and have studied at some of the finest universities in this country. I can say that in my experience there are no better books to read and study in the world than the Bible, the Book of Mormon, the Doctrine & Covenants, and the Pearl of Great Price. Make their teachings the standard by which you live!

In his last General Conference address, President Thomas S. Monson shared: "I implore each of us to prayerfully study and ponder the Book of Mormon each day. As we do so, we will **be in a position to hear the voice of the Spirit, to resist temptation, to overcome doubt and fear, and to receive heaven's help in our lives**." I know that these blessings are real as I have received each of them in my life.

This past year during a global pandemic, we have all learned the importance of clean hands. Have we also reflected on the importance of a pure heart to go with those clean hands? In this fallen world, we need immunity that extends beyond vaccines. Our current prophet (and former physician) President Russell M. Nelson has promised "that as you daily immerse yourself in the Book of Mormon, you can be immunized against the evils of the day." In this same October 2017 General Conference talk, President Nelson taught: "The truths in the Book of Mormon have the power to heal, comfort, restore, succor, strengthen, console, and cheer our souls." What timely prophetic promises!

If you have not already done so, make a commitment to read the scriptures – particularly the Book of Mormon – every day, every day, every day – for the rest of your life! I know that you and I will be blessed as we follow the counsel of modern prophets of God and read the Book of Mormon. I testify that God lives and loves each of us. This is the Church of Jesus Christ – and He leads it!

Chapter 1

Be Up and Doing:
Setting and Achieving Goals with Vision

"Jesus increased in wisdom and stature, and in favor with God and man."
– Luke 2:52

Setting goals and working to achieve them are key to success in life. We are here on earth to learn and improve and to prove ourselves (Abraham 3:25). This message was originally given in a stake conference priesthood leadership meeting in June 2017 and expanded upon in a December 2019 training meeting on the new Children and Youth Program.

I have enjoyed running throughout my life. In high school, I ran cross country and track. In college, I ran three marathons including the prestigious Boston Marathon. To be a good runner, you must be up and doing – before (in your preparation for) and during (in your performance of) the race.

A Marathon in Under Two Hours

Early in the morning of October 12, 2019, the greatest running achievement in my lifetime was accomplished in Vienna, Austria. For the first time in history, the marathon, a grueling race of 26.2 miles, was run in less than two hours (1:59:40.2) by a dedicated athlete from Kenya named Eliud Kipchoge. I watched this historic event live on YouTube – along with almost 400,000 other viewers from around the world. I came away inspired by the example of someone who truly understands what it means to be up and doing.

While you may never run a marathon, the story of how this accomplishment was achieved is worth studying and understanding.

Whatever goals you have in life, can and will be achieved by applying similar principles and strategies as Eliud Kipchoge.

Vision, Goals, Focus, and Tactical Plans

Five months before that historic day in Vienna, Eliud Kipchoge announced that he was going to break the two hour marathon barrier, an achievement that some thought would be impossible. Kipchoge took a photo next to a clock with the time 1:59:00 illustrating his vision for what he planned to accomplish. In meeting with the press, this athlete shared that achieving this feat would inspire others around the world and show us that "no human is limited."

Kipchoge surrounded himself with a dedicated team who shared his vision and desire to see him succeed. His wife and children encouraged him. Each week he went to a special training camp where he could focus. He only came home on the weekends. Daily and weekly goals were set, recorded, and shared over social media. Kipchoge was already the world record holder and reigning Olympic champion but he wanted to go faster. He put in hundreds and hundreds of miles over the weeks and months he prepared in order to build his stamina. Coaches and training partners pushed his speed and endurance.

On the day of the sub-two-hour attempt, a rotating pack of pacers surrounded Kipchoge to encourage and help him maintain the needed speed and consistency to reach his goal. A coach on a bicycle delivered water and energy drinks along the course. A pace car led the way with laser beams regularly striking the pavement to guide them on their path so that Kipchoge and his pacers could measure their progress and speed against a standard. New shoes provided spring to his step. In the end, the preparation and the pacing paid off and his seemingly impossible goal was achieved. This accomplishment is a reminder that "no human is limited."

The Application to All of Us

The principles and strategies used by Kipchoge can be used by all of us to achieve our goals as we are up and doing. Elder (now President) M. Russell Ballard taught in his April 2017 General Conference talk: "Over the years, I have observed that those who accomplish the most in this world are those with a **vision** for their lives, with **goals** to keep them **focus**ed on their vision and **tactical plans** for how to achieve them. Knowing where you are going and how you expect to get there can bring meaning, purpose, and accomplishment to life."

Elder Ballard continues: "Goal setting is essentially **beginning with the end in mind**. And planning is devising a way to get to that end. A key to happiness lies in **understanding what destinations truly matter**—and then spending our time, effort, and attention on the things that constitute a sure way to arrive there."

Example with My Own Goals

In 2017 I had two main personal goals: (1) to reduce my weight to <200 pounds and improve my physical fitness, and (2) to read and study the Book of Mormon and improve my spiritual fitness. In essence I was seeking a "mighty change in my heart" (Alma 5:14,26). *As I review my experiences in 2017, think about your own goals and your efforts to achieve them.*

Achieving a mighty change is to obtain a result that is meant to be permanent and last. To achieve this result requires consistent effort over time. We can only achieve and maintain a mighty change when we are "all in" as taught by Elder Gary Sabin of the Seventy in his April 2017 General Conference talk. Change comes through "small and simple things" that when done consistently over time result in "great things [being] brought to pass" (Alma 37:6). Are we working the equation from the right side (with a focus on results and purpose) or from the left side (where we are just setting goals)?

Prior to 2017, I had set significant weight loss as a goal every year for probably most of the last 15 or 20 years. So, what was different about my attempt in the first half of 2017? *I had vision and a real focus and desire to achieve my goal* of weight loss. I made my efforts a priority in my life. I lost more than 40 pounds in about six months and dropped my weight to well below 200 pounds.

Mentors and Examples

Elder Kim B. Clark of the Seventy visited our stake in December 2016 for our stake conference. His visit had a profound impact on me personally as I observed him up close. Elder Clark is very fit and spoke to the stake presidency about his efforts to exercise regularly. A few months earlier I had also attended a conference at Southern Virginia University where Elder Dallin H. Oaks spoke of his daily walks and efforts to maintain physical and spiritual fitness. I was inspired by the wonderful examples of fitness and commitment to daily exercise that I saw in both Elder Oaks and Elder Clark.

My doctor encouraged me in November 2016 to change my diet and get into better shape. My family also supported me in my goals. Thus, we succeed in our goals with advisors, mentors (examples), and support from family and friends.

Success comes when we (1) obtain and maintain vision, (2) establish goals and work towards them, (3) monitor progress daily, and (4) have patience and faith. Remember that by small and simple things great things are brought to pass (Alma 37:6). The *Lectures on Faith* teach that faith is the moving cause of all action. Exercise your faith and take action in whatever goals you think are worthy of pursuing.

Establish Vision

Vision must precede goals to achieve success. When this earth was created, vision and daily goals as well as returning and reporting progress helped make ideas a reality. Moses 3:5 states: "…For I, the Lord God, created all things of which I have spoken, spiritually, before they were naturally upon the face of the earth. Thus, a spiritual creation ("vision") preceded the physical creation ("goals").

In 2017 my desired weight loss came to pass because of a vision composed of three parts: (1) to be physically fit to enjoy life more, (2) to be in shape for a coming pioneer trek youth conference where I would need to walk 15 to 20 miles on the first day, and (3) to be able to run a 5k race with my son Marshall before he graduated from high school and to be able to run on my old high school track when I returned for my 30th high school reunion in June 2017.

Each morning as I exercised and throughout the day as I followed a careful diet, I had a mental image of running on my old high school track or covering the pioneer trek route without collapsing. These images, this vision, motivated me to succeed with my daily goals in 2017.

Set Simple Goals

Setting and achieving personal goals is the heart of the new *Children and Youth Program* that was introduced at the end of 2019. As we set meaningful goals in our lives and work to achieve them, we can experience mighty changes that will bless our lives. Jesus set the example of improving spiritually, physically, socially, and intellectually (see Luke 2:52). Improvements can come goal by goal in our lives.

In his April 2017 talk, Elder Ballard shared: "Experts on goal setting tell us that the simpler and more straightforward a goal is, the more power it will have. When we can reduce a goal to one clear image or one or two powerful and symbolic words, that goal can then become part of us and guide virtually everything we think and do."

When I was in high school, I put a notecard on a mirror in my bedroom that stated: "I want to be a state champion and I am willing to do the little things every day to get there!" Having a specific goal and being reminded of that goal daily helped me to eventually achieve this goal.

In my 2017 weight loss, I set an overall goal of losing about two pounds each week. Then I calculated how many calories I needed to achieve that goal. By simplifying my goals to specific daily amounts, I could focus my efforts and better take measurable action.

Measure Progress

To achieve success, you must measure your progress. There are a variety of tools that can be used to measure your progress depending on what your specific goal is.

To lose weight, I measured and recorded my weight every day. I also used an app (MyFitnessPal) to monitor everything I ate. A Fitbit tracked the number of steps I took. Creating an honest daily record enabled me to see and track my progress over time.

Elder Ballard in his April 2017 talk spoke about the importance of conducting regular personal private interviews. He shared: "…regularly take time to ask [yourself], 'How am I doing?' …who in this world knows you better than you know yourself? You know your thoughts, your private actions, your desires, and your dreams, goals, and plans. And you know better than anyone how you are progressing…"

We must regularly ask ourselves if we are spending our time in the right places to achieve our desired result. As a guide in tracking our spiritual progress, Elder Ballard encouraged reading and pondering the questions asked in Alma 5. Among these questions from Alma is one that touched me in my 2017 weight-loss journey: "Have [you] experienced [a] mighty change in your hearts?" (Alma 5:14). I experienced a "mighty change" with over a million steps as I logged hundreds of hours on our treadmill and walked and ran hundreds of flights of stairs in our home.

See a Mighty Change

The anatomy of a might change can be seen in the overall and daily weight loss I experienced over the first half of 2017. On Day 1 (November 29, 2016), I weighed 231.0 pounds. By Day 186 (June 2, 2017), my weight had been reduced to 190.0 pounds. I experienced a mighty change that came by small and simple daily weight reductions through diligent and consistent effort.

I find it interesting that under a parallel structuring of the Book of Alma, Alma 5 corresponds with Alma 37 (see Joseph M. Spencer, The structure of the Book of Alma, *Journal of Book of Mormon Studies* 2017, 26: 273-283). Thus, there is a scriptural correlation with a "mighty change" (Alma 5:14) being accomplished by "small and simple things" (Alma 37:6) over time.

The *Personal Development Youth Guidebook* emphasizes four parts in developing a pattern for growth. First, **discover** what you need to work on. Second, **plan** how you will do it. Third, **act** on your plan in faith. And, fourth, **reflect** on what you have learned.

Learn. Act. Share. Become!

The Duty to God program that existed in 2017 emphasized three principles: learn, act, and share.

Elder David A. Bednar of the Quorum of the Twelve Apostles wrote a series of three books about 10 years ago: (1) *Increase in Learning*, (2) *Act in Doctrine*, and (3) *Power to Become*. Together these books teach that as we learn and act on what we have learned we can gain power to become better. You might even be able to lose some weight or achieve another goal important to you. You might even be able to run a marathon faster than anyone else in history.

In *Increase in Learning*, Elder Bednar teaches that when we know "why" we will work harder to achieve the "what" and the "how". Doctrine teaches us the why, principles relate to what we need to do, and application help us understand how.

When you understand the doctrine of your true identity and purpose as a child of God, you will be have the strength to press forward through the difficulties of life. You will seek to improve. You will be up and doing.

Chapter 2

Revelation: Activate Your Spiritual Smart Phone and Call Home

"God shall give unto you knowledge by his Holy Spirit…"
– D&C 121:26

Learning to hear Him – to receive revelation from God – has been emphasized by a living prophet. To be up and doing and effective at ministering and serving one another, we must know how to receive and recognize revelation. As the world grows increasingly noisy, we must learn to hear His still, small voice. This message was shared in a stake conference general session in June 2018 and a stake priesthood meeting in October 2017.

Use Your Spiritual Smart Phone

When our daughter Amanda left for college at BYU Idaho, one of the last things my wife did was to purchase and activate a new smart phone for her. We wanted our daughter to be able to communicate with us when she was away from us because we love her. We wanted to be able to hear from her. We wanted to provide her with the ability to ask for and receive any advice from us that she needed at any time.

We were given the ability to call home as well when we left our heavenly home for our mortal "college" experience here on earth. Through prayer, we can communicate with our Heavenly Father to ask for and receive advice at any time as needed. The gift of the Holy Ghost and the scriptures represent the "spiritual smart phone" that our heavenly parents have given to us for communication with them. But a smart phone is of little value if we fail to use it or if we fail to charge it regularly, or if it breaks because we have not maintained it.

Why was it so important to my wife and I that our daughter have a working phone? Well, the previous semester her phone had broken shortly after she had gotten out to school – but she failed to tell us. We called her repeatedly. No answer. We became very anxious and worried about her. Finally, after more than a week of trying to reach her, we received an email from her explaining that her phone was not working and asking us to contact her roommate if we wanted to get in touch with her. She had gotten very busy and had not felt a need to call home. The battery in her phone was not working properly but she did not feel the need to fix it because she was getting along okay from her perspective.

Though it was surely frustrating at times, she was getting along without her phone and was just too busy to deal with getting it fixed or replaced. And too busy to even call her worried parents to get their help with it. Fortunately, there were no emergencies and our daughter survived that semester with an old flip phone that we mailed to her. Amanda's experience in not being able to call home for a while reminded me of an experience I had when I was a teenager that has forever stuck with me.

Failure to Call Home Leads to Missed Opportunities

In the summer before my senior year in high school, I came to Washington D.C. for the first time. This trip is when I fell in love with the D.C. area, which eventually led to me coming here for BYU's Washington Seminar program, for graduate school and for my career in forensic science.

In 1986, I was here at the University of Maryland for the National History Day competition because our project had won the Missouri state competition. My friends and I along with our history teacher and some chaperones enjoyed going into D.C. multiple days to see the Smithsonian museums and to visit Capitol Hill and other sites. I recall that we met our Missouri Congressman Tom Coleman and had a photo taken with him. It was a wonderful experience, but it could have been even better.

Unfortunately, we were so busy on our trip that I failed to call home the entire week we were in Washington D.C. My parents were a little disappointed when we got home that I had not checked in. In those days, we did not have cell phones and long-distance phone calls were expensive. Perhaps I justified my lack of communication with thinking that I would be saving my parents some money by not calling home.

What I did not learn until I got home was that my grandfather had arranged a special meeting for me and my friends with Senator Barry Goldwater, who was just completing his fifth term as senator from Arizona and was at the time one of the most powerful people on Capitol Hill. Senator Goldwater and my grandfather had been fraternity brothers at the University of Arizona and were lifelong friends. Because of my failure to call home while I was in Washington D.C., I missed a unique opportunity to meet an interesting person. Senator Goldwater retired from the U.S. Senate about six months after our visit – and so the meeting that had been arranged and could have happened, never did.

This lost opportunity was an important lesson to me in my life. Since then, I have never failed to call home and check in when I am traveling. The call does not need to be long, but I have learned that regular communication with home is critical. Likewise, we need to daily pray and read our scriptures to maintain regular communication with our heavenly home.

Over the years, I have reflected on how my experience with visiting Washington D.C. as a teenager for the first time is like our mortal experience here on earth. There are wonderful things to see and do here while we are in mortality and sometimes we may get too busy to call home and check in with our Heavenly Father. He may have arranged for us to meet some interesting people or to serve someone in need. However, because we fail to check in through regular prayer and scripture study, we may miss opportunities to receive revelation and meet interesting people that we may be inspired to help.

The Gift of the Holy Ghost

The greatest gift that Heavenly Father can give us in this life is the ability to receive revelation – to enjoy communication from Him. He has given each of us a "spiritual smart phone." When a member of the Church of Jesus Christ of Latter-day Saints is baptized and then confirmed, the gift of the Holy Ghost is bestowed upon them. Think for a moment what is said during the confirmation. The individual being confirmed is invited to "receive the Holy Ghost". Thus**, the very first invitation what someone is given after becoming a member of the Church is to receive revelation** – to activate our spiritual smart phone to be able to communicate with heaven.

The Prophet Joseph Smith explained: "No [one] can receive the Holy Ghost without receiving revelation. The Holy Ghost is a revelator." (TPJS, p. 328)

More recently Elder David A. Bednar of the Quorum of the Twelve Apostles has taught: "Taking 'the Holy Spirit for [our] guide' (D&C 45:57) is possible and is essential for our spiritual growth and survival in an increasingly wicked world. Sometimes as Latter-day Saints we talk and act as though recognizing the influence of the Holy Ghost in our lives is the rare or exceptional event. We should remember, however, that the covenant promise is *that we may always have His Spirit to be with us.* This supernal blessing applies to every single member of the Church who has been baptized, confirmed, and instructed to 'receive the Holy Ghost.'" (April 2006 General Conference)

Unfortunately, I think we are living beneath our privileges and many people are not actively seeking to receive revelation. Failure to receive revelation from heaven can come because of one of three possible reasons: (1) **we do not seek it** – in other words we are not trying to call home because we are too busy or think we are doing okay on our own, (2) **we are not worthy** – perhaps because we have not maintained our spiritual smart phone and have permitted it to break just as we might break commandments that distance us from the Spirit's guiding influence in our lives, or (3) **we do not know how to receive or recognize it**.

I want to spend the remainder of my talk on the third point – how to receive and recognize revelation from God.

Knowledge from Heaven

I enjoy looking for patterns in the scriptures. One of my favorite patterns to study are "if-then" formulas. These occur when the scriptures record that "if" you do something, "then" God promises you something. These "if-then" statements are "covenants" or promises from God. God has promised that when we do what He says, then He is bound – He is required – to deliver the gift or blessing to us that we have qualified ourselves to receive (see D&C 82:10).

I love D&C Sections 121, 122, and 123. I grew up in northwest Missouri. In fact, my stake center was about three miles from the Liberty Jail where these sections of the Doctrine & Covenants were written on March 20 and March 22, 1839.

I can recall how bitter cold the winters can be in Missouri. I remember a few times in high school when the wind chill got down to -70 degrees Fahrenheit. When I consider the fact that D&C 121 was given to and recorded by the Prophet Joseph Smith after he had been imprisoned in a cold, dark jail in Western Missouri for four long winter months, I am even more amazed and appreciative of the beautiful language and insights that we have in these scriptures that were received during a time of terrible challenges. Here then is another lesson about revelation. **Revelation comes when we need it in times of trouble.**

D&C 121:26 states: "God shall give unto you knowledge by his Holy Spirit, yea, by the unspeakable gift of the Holy Ghost." D&C 121:33 further teaches us that "the Almighty [desires to pour] down knowledge from heaven upon the heads of the Latter-day Saints." Knowledge from heaven is a beautiful description of revelation. So, what is the formula for the flow of this revelation – this "knowledge from heaven"? Let's look for the "if-then" statements. We find them in the remaining verses of D&C 121.

Starting in verse 34: "Behold, there are many called [including those who have been confirmed members of the Church and have been invited to receive the Holy Ghost], but few are chosen. In other words, few have chosen to receive revelation the way that God intended them to do so. They have failed to activate their spiritual smart phones or to call, to listen to, and to receive knowledge from heaven.

Now, let us examine the formula for receiving this flow of revelation – this "knowledge from heaven":

From verse 35, we are taught **the importance of putting God first in our lives**. Our hearts cannot be set so much upon the things of this world and the honors of men.

From verse 36, we are admonished to **be worthy – to be righteous and obedient –** because the powers of heaven – including revelation – come only through principles of righteousness.

From verses 37 through 45, we are reminded **to repent** and **to be humble and grateful** and **to be kind and charitable to others**. We cannot seek to cover our sins or gratify our pride and our vain ambitions. We must be long-suffering, gentle, meek, kind, and allow our whole souls to be full of charity towards all people.

From verse 45 with the phrase "let virtue garnish your thoughts unceasingly", we are taught that **revelation flows through clean minds and worthy people**. Just like electrical power can only flow through clean and uncorroded wires, likewise our minds and our spirits must be clear and clean to receive knowledge and power from heaven. To me, this is why keeping the Sabbath day holy is crucial and partaking worthily of the sacrament each week is essential to being clean before God – so that we are ready to receive revelation.

Those are the "ifs" – the requirements God is asking of us to receive blessings from Him. Now, let us look for the "then" statements to see the blessings that are promised. We find the word "then" in the middle of verse 45. The blessings available to us are clearly stated in the second half of verse 45 and all of verse 46: "*Then* shall thy confidence wax strong in the presence of God; and the doctrine of the priesthood shall distil upon thy soul as the dews from heaven. The Holy Ghost shall be thy constant companion, and thy scepter an unchanging scepter of righteousness and truth; and thy dominion shall be an everlasting dominion, and without compulsory means it [meaning revelation] shall flow unto thee forever and ever."

Learning to Receive Revelation

About three months after D&C 121 was recorded, Joseph Smith described revelation as coming as "sudden strokes of ideas, so that by noticing it, you may find it fulfilled the same day or soon; [in other words] those things that were presented unto your minds by the Spirit of God, will come to pass; and thus by learning the Spirit of God and understanding it, you may grow into the principle of revelation." (TPJS p. 151)

We must learn to understand the Spirit of God. We can learn to receive revelation by experiencing it. This takes time and experience.

The process of receiving revelation begins by asking a question of God with real intent. Note that D&C 121 begins with a question by Joseph Smith – "O God, where art thou?" (D&C 121:1). As a 14-year old boy, young Joseph sought guidance from God in the Sacred Grove with another question: "Which church should I join?"

What questions do you have?

Our living prophet, President Russell M. Nelson, in April 2018 General Conference (April 2018, Sunday morning) taught us how to receive revelation. He said: "The Prophet Joseph Smith set a pattern for us to follow in resolving our questions. Drawn to the promise of James that if we lack wisdom we may ask of God, the boy Joseph took his question directly to Heavenly Father. He sought personal revelation, and his seeking opened this last dispensation. In like manner, what will your seeking open for you? What wisdom do you lack? What do you feel an urgent need to know or understand? Follow the example of the Prophet Joseph. Find a quiet place where you can regularly go. Humble yourself before God. Pour out your heart to your Heavenly Father. Turn to Him for answers and for comfort. Pray in the name of Jesus Christ about your concerns, your fears, your weaknesses – yes, the very longing of your heart. And then listen! Write the thoughts that come to your mind. Record your feelings and follow through with actions that you are prompted to take. As you repeat this process day after day, month after month, year after year, you will 'grow into the principle of revelation.'"

Some Principles of Revelation that I Have Learned

May I quickly share a few insights I have learned over the years regarding revelation.

1) **The process of receiving revelation begins by asking a question of God with real intent**. Real intent means that you are willing to act when an answer is received.

2) **The Lord expects us to do our homework**. As President Nelson taught in this last conference: "I know that good inspiration is based upon good information." What price have you paid in preparing to receive revelation? Have you studied the topic and the options out before you have taken the matter to the Lord?

3) **We must learn to listen to the still small voice**. To hear it, we must reduce the noise of the world. Revelation comes likes the dews from heaven. For me, feelings of peace and specific thoughts distill upon my soul in the early morning

hours. For my wife, she feels the Spirit best in the quiet of the night when the day's work is done and others have gone to bed. We may each feel the Spirit differently. The most important thing we can do is to learn to receive revelation. I am sometimes awoken in the morning by specific thoughts. I often drive to work in my car in silence reflecting on things I have read that morning in the scriptures. I have found that the Lord can teach me and reach me if I am not distracted by the radio. Find your quiet place and take time to ponder each day.

4) **We should take notes on what we learn** so that we do not forget what the Lord is teaching us. Not long after we were married my wife purchased a special notebook for me in which I have recorded my testimony and other experiences I have had in learning from the Spirit. I call this notebook my "small plates of Nephi" because it contains "the things of my soul" (2 Nephi 4:15).

5) **Reading revelation will bring revelation.** Reading the scriptures and especially the Book of Mormon every day opens the door to revelation on any subject that the Lord wishes to speak to you (see Elder Oaks, *Ensign* January 1995). Prophets have invited us to seek answers through the power of the Spirit that comes from diligent scripture study. We need to ponder what we read and apply the message to us and our needs.

6) **When you receive revelation, take action!** The Lord will continue to teach you if He knows He can trust you. We must step into the darkness, trust Him and allow Him to use us to do His work. Like Nephi, we must be willing to "go and do" (1 Nephi 3:7).

7) **Revelation comes line upon line**. Remember that the entire picture is not revealed at once. Rather as 2 Nephi 28:30 explains, the Lord teaches us line upon line and precept upon precept. "For behold, thus said the Lord God: I will give unto the children of men line upon line, precept upon precept, here a little and there a little; and blessed are those who hearken unto my precepts, and lend an ear unto my counsel, for they shall learn wisdom [i.e., develop a relationship with God]; for unto him that receiveth I will give more; and from them that shall say, We have enough, from them shall be taken away even that which they have."

8) **Revelation is non-transferable** (see *Of All Things! Classic Quotations from Hugh Nibley*, p. 233). It is personal to you and to your sphere of influence.

Joseph Smith on the Gift of the Holy Ghost

About six months after leaving the Liberty Jail where section 121 was written, the Prophet Joseph Smith made his first visit to Washington D.C. He was here in our nation's capital to seek help in getting compensation for the land stolen from the Mormons when they were forced to flee Missouri. In December 1839, he came to Capitol Hill and met with some senators. *By the way, in case you were wondering, Barry Goldwater was not one of them...*

Joseph Smith had the opportunity to meet Martin van Buren, who was then President of the United States. A letter written home by Joseph's traveling companion, Elias Higbee, shares some interesting insights about the importance of the gift of the Holy Ghost in our lives as it applied to their visit. Brother Higbee records: "In our interview with the President [of the United States], he interrogated us wherein we differed in our religion from the other religions of the day. Brother Joseph said we differed in mode of baptism, and the gift of the Holy Ghost by the laying on of hands. We considered that all other considerations were contained in the gift of the Holy Ghost." (*History of the Church* 4:42)

To me what is being taught in this statement is that revelation, which occurs through the gift of the Holy Ghost, is an essential part of the Restored Gospel of Jesus Christ. The Prophet Joseph later taught: "We believe that the holy men of old spake as they were moved by the Holy Ghost, and that holy men in these days speak by the same principle; we believe in [the Holy Ghost] being a comforter and a witness bearer, that it brings things past to our remembrance, leads us into all truth, and shows us of things to come; we believe that 'no man can know that Jesus is the Christ, but by the Holy Ghost.' [see 1 Corinthians 12:3]" (*History of the Church* 5:27)

Perhaps the most important revelation that we each need to receive in our life is a personal testimony of our Savior Jesus Christ and a witness that He has restored His Church to the earth again through the Prophet Joseph Smith and that we are led by living prophets, seers, and revelators today. This knowledge from heaven will be a great blessing and support in the days ahead and is essential to our salvation.

Hearing the Spirit's Signal above the World's Noise

In the fall of 2017, my office did a press release for a project I had just started at work. There arose was a flurry of opposition from people who do not want this project done because they are afraid of what might be uncovered. I work on forensic science topics that can show up in the news and can be contentious in the adversarial environment that exists in courts of law. Maintaining focus and moving forward with our project was challenging with loud noises of opposition coming from a few vocal critics. Ultimately we pressed forward and succeeded, but for a time it was hard to do so. I learned a lot about noise from this experience and the interference it causes.

Noise from the world impacts our ability to receive the Spirit's signal. About 25 years ago, Elder Boyd K. Packer of the Quorum of the Twelve Apostles shared in General Conference (October 1991, "Reverence Invites Revelation"):

> "The world grows increasingly noisy. Clothing and grooming and conduct are looser and sloppier and more disheveled. Raucous music, with obscene lyrics blasted through amplifiers while lights flash psychedelic colors, characterizes the drug culture. Variations of these things are gaining wide acceptance and influence over our youth.

> "Doctors even say that our physical sense of hearing can be permanently damaged by all of this noise.

> "This trend to more noise, more excitement, more contention, less restraint, less dignity, less formality is not coincidental nor innocent nor harmless.

> "The first order issued by a commander mounting a military invasion is the jamming of the channels of communication of those he intends to conquer.

> "Irreverence suits the purposes of the adversary by obstructing the delicate channels of revelation in both mind and spirit."

Elder Packer powerfully concludes: "No one of us can survive in the world of today, much less in what it soon will become, without personal inspiration."

Being connected to the internet can be important for work activities or obtaining information at home or school. Most of us have probably experienced the frustration of losing WiFi signal on our smart phone, laptop, or other digital device and being unable to connect to the internet for a brief period of time. There are a number of reasons why loss of signal happens. Consider what can be done to gain a stronger signal so that we can receive the information that we need.

Signal Amplification

I have spent my scientific career measuring DNA molecules that are too small to be seen by the naked eye and even by sophisticated instruments. The DNA signal must be amplified before it can be seen. Scripture study amplifies and strengthens the Spirit's signal. Reading revelation helps us receive revelation.

To increase the Spirit's signal, we can close the distance – get nearer to God. How do we do this? We read the Book of Mormon every day, every day, every day! President Spencer W. Kimball stated: "I find that when I get casual in my relationships with divinity and when it seems that no divine ear is listening and no divine voice is speaking, that I am far, far away. If I immerse myself in the scriptures the distance narrows and the spirituality returns." (*Teachings of Presidents of the Church: Spencer W. Kimball* (2006), p. 67)

Reduce the Noise

The Spirit does not shout to get our attention. 1 Kings 19:11-12 describes the prophet Elijah feeling a great and strong wind, an earthquake, a fire. But the Lord was not in any of them. Finally, "a still small voice" brought an important message from the Lord to His prophet. Likewise, the Lamanites who had imprisoned Nephi and Lehi in the land of Nephi around 30 B.C. heard a voice from heaven inviting them to repent and to listen to the Lord's messengers. Helaman 5:30 describes the Spirit's voice as "not a voice of thunder" nor "a voice of a great tumultuous noise" but rather as "a still voice of perfect mildness, as if it had been a whisper, and it did pierce even to the very soul."

The Lord told the Brother of Jared: "My Spirit will not always strive with man..." (Ether 2:15). Sins are noise and jam the Spirit's signal. Digital distractions and spending too much time playing video games are noise to our spiritual lives. Viewing pornography brings noise. All aspects of noise can drown out or block signal. The noise of the world can block the signal we want to receive from heaven. D&C 121:45-46 – "Let virtue garnish thy thoughts unceasingly; then shall they confidence wax strong in the presence of God... The Holy Ghost shall be thy constant companion..."

Take time to ponder each day. Quiet the noise in our lives. Unplug for a few minutes. Distractions can prevent us from receiving and understanding the signal being sent.

Act on Knowledge Received

We must receive, record, and act on the signal we receive. It is not enough to just hear the message of the Book of Mormon and of the Restoration – we must live it and apply the teachings in our lives to achieve the full benefits available to us. "Living the message of the gospel brings conversion" (Scott Esplin, *Living the Book of Mormon*, p. 45).

We have in the introduction to the Book of Mormon a statement made by the Prophet Joseph Smith in 1841: "I told the brethren that the Book of Mormon was the most correct of any book on earth, and the keystone of our religion, and a man would get nearer to God by abiding by its precepts, than by any other book." This statement was made on November 28, 1841 when the Prophet Joseph met with the Nauvoo City Council and members of the Quorum of the Twelve Apostles. Also in attendance was Brother Joseph Fielding, who had just returned from serving four years as a missionary in England where he had used the Book of Mormon in teaching and converting people to the Gospel of Jesus Christ.

Thus, Joseph Smith made this famous statement in what was effectively a stake priesthood meeting held 176 years ago where a missionary report was being given.

I would invite each of you to take time and ponder the following question: *How have I gotten closer to God this year from following the invitation of my leaders to read the Book of Mormon?*

Power from Heaven

We can be connected to heaven in a powerful way as we daily study the Book of Mormon. President Ezra Taft Benson taught: "There is a power in the book which will begin to flow into your lives the moment you begin a serious study of the book. You will find greater power to resist temptation. You will find the power to avoid deception. You will find the power to stay on the strait and narrow path. The scriptures are called "the words of life" (see D&C 84:85), and nowhere is that more true than it is of the Book of Mormon. When you being to hunger and thirst after those words, you will find life in greater and greater abundance." (*A Witness and a Warning*, p. 21-22).

I offer my witness – my expert witness – from more than 30 years of personal experience in careful study of the Book of Mormon. The signal from heaven will be amplified and we will receive the guidance and direction we desire in our lives. We will be able to rise above the noise of the world and hear the word of the Lord to us personally.

The heavens are open. There is signal constantly coming from a loving Heavenly Father who very much wants to connect with us. For us to hear Him, we must reduce the noise and distractions of the world. We must get nearer to God. We must be open to receive the messages that He wants to share with us. Reading and searching the Book of Mormon every day opens our communication channels with heaven. I know from many, many personal experiences that this is true. I invite you to find out for yourselves – to experiment upon the word (Alma 32:27) and get nearer to God.

Revelation Is Real

We are invited to seek communication with God and to receive revelation and inspiration from Him. Revelation is real! I know because I have received it. I also know that a loving Heavenly Father wants us to call home through prayer on a regular basis so that we do not miss opportunities to meet interesting people and have experiences that He has uniquely prepared for us as we minister to others.

Chapter 3

The Rod, the Path, and the Tree: Coming Unto Christ

"they…caught hold of the end of the rod of iron; and…did press their way forward"
– 1 Nephi 8:30

When you are up and doing, it is important to consider the direction are you heading and what you use to guide your efforts. This message is from a stake conference adult session in December 2018.

The rod, the path, and the tree
Images and symbols with special meaning to me
Recorded by Nephi and Lehi – Book of Mormon prophets of old
Who through their dreams and their writings powerfully foretold
How we can get through our challenging journeys in life
To survive with our families in a world full of conflict and strife.

We are invited to continually hold to the iron rod
To study the scriptures, which are the word of God
Press forward, onward and upward we head towards the tree
Looking forward to wonderful reunions and joyful jubilee
When we arrive at the base of the tree
Will we fall down and humbly bow our knee?
And there proclaim our gratitude and love
For our Savior and Redeemer, and our Father above?

Our prophet has invited us to walk this covenant path
So that we can gain all that our Heavenly Father hath
For the tree of life represents the temple you see
We must make a greater effort to go and to do and to be.

Hear the call of our prophet
And the invitation of our Savior
The rod, the path, and the tree
Hold fast, stay on, and come unto Me!

Symbols from Lehi's Tree of Life Dream

The **rod of iron** serves both as a guide rail and a guard rail to assist us as we travel through the mists of darkness and as we try to avoid falling into the **filthy water** that runs the entire length of the covenant path. The **mists of darkness**, which are temptations of the devil (1 Nephi 12:17), can distort our views of the path with visual noise. Occupants of the nearby **great and spacious building**, which symbolizes the pride of the world (1 Nephi 11:36), attempt to disrupt our journey with loud, mocking voices (1 Nephi 8:27). Their scorning generates verbal noise that we must cope with to reach the tree and the happiness that awaits us there as we partake of its fruit. Finally, to me, the covenant path represents a home-centered effort of daily gospel study and learning that enables each of us to eventually return to our heavenly home to partake of **the fruit of the tree**, which is eternal life.

This journey through mortal life to eternal life is made possible by our Savior Jesus Christ who declared in John 14:6 that **He is the way** (the covenant path), **the truth** (the scriptures or rod of iron), and **the life** (the goal of eternal life = tree).

The Prophet Beckons Us from a Position by the Tree

The prophet has a different viewpoint of the elements in Lehi's dream. I found it interesting in my recent study of 1 Nephi 8 that Lehi explains his entire dream from a vantage point of being by the tree. In verse 19, Lehi describes the rod of iron, which "led to the tree by which I stood." In verse 20, he comments on the strait and narrow path, which leads to "the tree by which I stood." In verse 21, Lehi notes many people "pressing forward, that they might obtain the path which led unto the tree by which I stood." The rod, the path, and the tree. Hold fast, stay on, and come unto Me!

President Nelson followed this same pattern when he first spoke to us on January 16, 2018 as the new President of the Church of Jesus Christ of Latter-day Saints. He spoke to us from inside the Salt Lake Temple. President Nelson, like Lehi, has invited each of us to hold to the rod and keep on the covenant path that leads us to the tree of life.

In his October 2018 talk for the Women's Session of General Conference, President Nelson extended four invitations. You may find it interesting how these invitations match 1 Nephi 8 elements.

First, participate in a 10-day fast from social media so that we can tune out noise coming from the great and spacious building. Second, read the Book of Mormon and mark references to the Savior so that we can hold fast to the rod of iron. Third, establish a pattern of regular temple attendance and seek to *know* more, to *understand* more, to *feel* more about temples than you ever have before. In other words, come to the tree of life and partake of its fruit. And fourth, participate fully in Relief Society [and we might add home-centered gospel learning] so that we can keep on the covenant path.

Symbolism of the Tree of Life

The tree of life can be symbolic of many things – and certainly the temple is one of them. While seeing baby Jesus in vision, Nephi was taught that the tree of life represented the love of God (1 Nephi 11:20-22). To his unbelieving brothers, however, Nephi simply explains that the tree of life is the tree of life. This was not a particularly helpful answer in my opinion, but it seemed to satisfy them.

For those who have eyes to see and ears to hear, Nephi explains in 1 Nephi 11:7 that the tree is the Son of God. This knowledge comes to Nephi because he was desirous to see, and hear, and know of these things for himself (1 Nephi 10:17).

Nephi gains this knowledge by visiting the temple. As is explained at the beginning of 1 Nephi 11, Nephi went "into an exceedingly high mountain", which would be equivalent today of us going to the temple. Nephi even experienced a temple recommend interview from the Spirit when he is asked: "Believest thou that thy father saw the tree of which he hath spoken?" (1 Nephi 11:4). Nephi responds: "Yea, thou knowest that I believe all the words of my father" (1 Nephi 11:5). The door of knowledge then opens, and Nephi is shown in vision the birth, baptism, ministry, and crucifixion of the Lamb of God.

As we are up and doing, we move along the covenant path through firming holding to the rod of iron. In time, we will come forth and fall down and partake of the fruit of the tree (1 Nephi 8:30) and experience eternal blessings that will fill our souls with "exceeding great joy" (1 Nephi 8:12).

Chapter 4

Prepare for Your Temple Blessings

"prepare every needful thing; and establish…a house of glory, …a house of God"
– D&C 88:119

To be up and doing involves moving along the covenant path, which will lead to the temple and wonderful blessings available to you. What are you doing to prepare now for your temple blessings? This message was delivered in the general session of stake conference in December 2020. Portions were also prepared for a stake high priest quorum meeting held in September 2018.

Moroni and the Blessings of the Temple

I am grateful for Moroni and his vital role in bringing us the Book of Mormon. With 1,400 years to prepare for his initial visit with young Joseph Smith, what was the first message that Moroni shared?

According to Joseph Smith-History 1:36, after explaining about the Book of Mormon record, Moroni first quoted Malachi 3:1 (which states in part "…the Lord, whom ye seek, shall suddenly come to his <u>temple</u>…") and then Moroni shared a different version of Malachi 4:5-6 as is recorded in Doctrine & Covenants Section 2 ("…I will reveal unto you the Priesthood, by the hand of Elijah the prophet…" [why? so that] …the <u>hearts of the children shall turn to their fathers</u>…"). So what was Moroni's very first message? *The importance and blessings of temple and family history work!*

A statue of Moroni is found on temples spires around the world. Have you considered why Moroni? Why not the angel Gabriel who announced the birth of Jesus Christ or the prophet Elijah who restored priesthood keys and the sealing power that is used in the temple? On our temples, Moroni is depicted with a trumpet, which symbolizes his desire to share an important message with the world.

I found some insights on Moroni in a 1978 *Ensign* article[1]: "With the loss of his father and his people, Moroni inherited a burden of loneliness virtually unparalleled in human history…Moroni's opening words in Mormon chapter 8 are [filled] with an infinite sorrow: '*I am alone.* My father hath been slain in battle, and all my kinsfolk, and I have not friends nor whither to go…' (Mormon 8:5, emphasis added). …" *One of the lessons to me during this COVID-19 pandemic is that I have gained a better appreciation for the impact of being separated from those you love.*

The article continues: "Moroni's years of isolation from the family of men must have deepened his appreciation for the eternal family and his awareness of the significance of temple work. Much of what Moroni told the young Joseph Smith during their first encounter takes on added meaning in this context… Only someone in Moroni's position, cut off in time from both ancestors and descendants, could begin to appreciate the unspeakable loneliness of being left eternally with 'neither root nor branch'…"

I am so thankful that priesthood power is available today and used in temples to bind families for eternity! We are not alone as we turn our hearts to our ancestors!

---

[1] See Brother Cole Durham, *Ensign* June 1978, pp. 56-61, available at https://www.churchofjesuschrist.org/study/ensign/1978/06/moroni?lang=eng

Why the Temple Matters to Me and to You

A former temple president recently shared[2]: "While baptism focuses on the *cleansing* of the soul, the temple focuses on the *development* of the soul." I love that idea. The temple develops our souls.

While conducting temple recommend interviews with members of our stake, I sometimes ask them to share their perspectives on the blessings of the temple. A good friend recorded and shared more than 64 blessings from his temple experiences.

I have tried to incorporate what I learned from these discussions into a poem that expresses my deep love for the temple and its blessings.

> The holy temple is a house of God
> A place of beauty and love, where I am filled with awe
> Each time I go there to serve and learn
> I come away blessed with greater concern
> For my sisters and brothers – my eternal family dear
> I am filled with hope and comfort and cheer
> For a temple is hallowed ground where angels softly tread
> As we seek and serve our precious kindred dead.

> As we come to the temple to unite our families there
> We will receive strength and wisdom to better bear
> The challenges of life we all most certainly face
> As we work to make this world a better place
> When we are converted and know our Heavenly Parents care
> Will we return often to the temple and visit Them there?

---

[2] Elder Bruce C. Hafen in an Interpreter Book of Moses conference (YouTube https://www.youtube.com/watch?v=VWUWMZN-5fA&t=1502s, ~38 minutes into the 1:36:56 video)

In the holy temple, heaven and earth connect
Wisdom flows, peace abounds, and we are a little more perfect!
As saviors on Mount Zion, our family history efforts we bring
And our hearts to our ancestors do swing
Their praises for us through eternity will ring
As together we acknowledge our Savior as prophet, priest, and king!

I invite you to reflect on blessings you have personally experienced in the temple. Write these blessings down and share them with your family and friends.

Your Temple Recommend Opens the Gates of Heaven

A bishop shared the following perspective with me: "One of the greatest blessings of the temple is the journey an individual makes to the temple recommend. These good people learn to repent and to change. Your recommend is a demonstration to the Lord of your worthiness. You need your recommend every day of your life. Young missionaries receive a mission tag and a temple recommend – but only the temple recommend is required to enter the presence of God." This good bishop concluded: "As for prospective and returned missionaries, I am not as concerned about the tag that will be or used to be on your shirt as I am the recommend in your pocket."

Temple recommends provide the means to unlock the gates of heaven and to demonstrate to ourselves and to our Father in Heaven that we are progressing on the covenant path. In a stake presidency message sent in November 2020, we expressed that it is the deepest desire of our hearts to have every youth and adult of our stake, be worthy to enter the temple – and to perform proxy ordinances for their kindred dead. This invitation is timeless.

I know from experience that as we turn our hearts to our ancestors on the other side of the veil, we will grow in love for them as well as those around us on this side of the veil. On our first wedding anniversary more than 25 years ago, my wife and I spent the day in the Washington DC Temple. Our love for one another grew as we performed proxy baptisms, confirmations, initiatory ordinances, endowments, and sealings for my second great uncle and his family. I can still recall the feelings of that wonderful day as we ascended from the basement baptistry to the sixth floor sealing room. We came closer to God, to our ancestors, and to each other through performing this service in the temple.

In his closing remarks as part of the October 2019 General Conference, President Russell M. Nelson stated: "…the crowning jewel of the Restoration is the holy temple. Its sacred ordinances and covenants are pivotal to preparing a people who are ready to welcome the Savior at His Second Coming…" President Nelson continued: "…the blessings of the temple are available to any and all people who will prepare themselves. But before they can enter a dedicated temple, they need to qualify. The Lord wants all His children to partake of the eternal blessings available in His temple. He has directed what each person must do to qualify to enter His holy house… All requirements to enter the temple relate to personal holiness." And then, President Nelson reviewed the 15 questions asked as part of a temple recommend.

I invite you to review these questions as part of a regular, ongoing personal assessment. You do not have to wait for an interview with a member of your ward bishopric and stake presidency to know your standing before the Lord.

Prepare for Your Temple Blessings

Show the Lord that you value the temple through obtaining and always maintaining an active temple recommend. Find the names of ancestors that you can take with you when go next to the temple.

A friend shared how she is trying to make the temple more "present" right now. She is fasting and praying for temples to reopen. She has washed and ironed her temple clothes. She even repeats in her mind as much of the temple covenant language as she can remember. Doing these small and simple things have brought the spirit of the temple into her life now. She is an excellent example of following President Nelson's invitation to the sisters in October 2018 General Conference to "seek to *know* more, to *understand* more, to *feel* more about temples than you ever have before."

Even when I am unable to attend a temple as regularly as I may want, I study and ponder the marvelous blessings of the temple. I look forward to the day when I can personally thank Moroni for his role in the coming forth of the Book of Mormon and in the restoration of temple blessings. *We will not be alone in the eternities!*

Temple Recommend Insights

As a member of the stake presidency, I conduct more than 100 temple recommends each year. The following are some of the insights I have gained in reflecting on the temple recommend questions and process:
- The interview is personal, private, and conducted one-by-one; it is an opportunity to model a connection to the Savior and to reflect on how He loves each of us individually and that in a future day we will each have our own personal interview with the Lord one-by-one

- In some ways, temple recommend interviews foreshadow the interview we will have on judgment day before our Savior; the temple recommend interview is an opportunity to prepare us for that day

- There is symbolism in the paper recommend itself with the three signatures representing ordinances performed in the temple

- The interview itself can be an extension of the temple where revelation is received and shared!

- People come with different levels of preparation, just like they do to the temple; sadly, some do not dress for an interview like they would if they were going into the temple!; this is something we can teach and remind people of → that the temple recommend interview is an extension of the temple and is conducted with an authorized representative of the Lord who is on His errand when performing the interview

- Priesthood key holders or their counselor representatives stand as sentinel angels in conducting interviews; in fact, the spires on the Washington DC Temple represent exactly that function – the three spires on the west side represent the bishop and his counselors in their Aaronic Priesthood leadership function and the three spires on the east side represent the stake presidency in their Melchizedek Priesthood leadership role; thus, the spire topped by Moroni presents our stake president in his role as the chief priesthood key holder for our stake who trumpets an invitation for all to come unto Christ – to gather Israel on both sides of the veil

- Our responses to the temple recommend questions are a form of bearing testimony – in our responses, we reaffirm our commitment to the covenants we have made; we make this declaration to ourselves, to God, and to His angel witnesses (the two interviewers who figuratively stand as sentinel angels)

- The 15 questions begin with doctrine and move to application – just like the Articles of Faith

- The beginning questions are presented in the same order as the "Come, Follow Me" topics that have been part of the youth curriculum from 2013 to 2019 [January is the Godhead, February is the Plan of Salvation, March is the Atonement of Jesus Christ, April is the Restoration, May is Prophets and Revelation, and June is Priesthood and Priesthood Keys]; thus, the "Come, Follow Me" teaching pattern is designed to prepare our youth for and to point them towards the temple! Youth are taught in the same order each year, which order corresponds to the first four temple recommend questions

- The questions demonstrate what is needed to have faith as defined in the Lectures on Faith; first, a knowledge of God and His true character; just as the Articles of Faith begin with teaching us the true nature of the Godhead – that the Father, the Son, and the Holy Ghost are three separate and distinct beings with a united purpose, so also the first temple recommend question assesses our appreciation for this knowledge; second, we must know that God has power to act and to save us if we are to have faith in Him; hence the second question, which relates to the Atonement of Christ and His power to save and redeem us

- John 17:3 states that life eternal comes from knowing the Godhead, which is where the first question starts – with the end goal in mind – to gain eternal life and return to Their presence

- John 14:6 indicates that the Way back to our heavenly home is through the Atoning sacrifice of our Savior, which is the purpose of the second question

- D&C 21:1,4 teaches that we learn about our Savior today because of the Restoration began through the Prophet Joseph Smith and continued through living prophets, seers, and revelators today, hence the purpose for questions 3 and 4

- The questions asked in temple recommend interviews correlate to covenants made in the temple, and each question thus serves as a protection for those not yet ready to make and keep sacred covenants

- In a similar manner, baptismal interviews precede initial covenant making and the questions there are also for the applicant's protection to keep them from taking on more than they are willing and able to bear (see Mosiah 18:8-10)

- Temple recommend questions are repeated (with exactness) once by a bishopric member and then again by a stake presidency member; this is teaching a pattern of learning that is amplified further throughout the endowment ceremony; repetition helps us remember revelation

- The questions can represent temporal and spiritual aspects of our testimonies and commitments – much like we are taught about the Creation being both spiritual and temporal in nature that represent two phases: planning and execution of the plan

- Other ordinances of the Gospel similarly reflect temporal and spiritual aspects, such as baptism and confirmation and the bread and the water in the sacrament we partake each week

- The temple garment statement has a connection to the initiatory ordinance; this statement should to be read or reviewed with each individual interviewed as a reminder of what is probably the most tangible and daily aspect of temple worship, the proper wearing of the garment which represents our commitment to the Savior and the blessings of His atoning sacrifice for us

- One of my interviewees asked about the history of the temple recommend questions; I did not know the answer to her question and so I researched the topic and came to find out that commitment to paying tithing has been a recommend question from the beginning of this dispensation[3]; the promise in Malachi 3:10 of the windows of heaven opening to us when we pay our tithing has taken on new meaning to me; the ability to enter and worship in the temple enables this promise to be fulfilled as temples become a place of revelation where the windows of heaven open and we hear and see what the God of heaven wants to share with us through His Holy Spirit; paying tithing leads to temple blessings and personal revelation; I know this pattern to be true for I have experienced it many times

- Why are there strict standards of worthiness to enter the House of the Lord? Why are we requested to ask questions with exactness? Simply put, it is His House not ours! The Lord of Hosts sets the requirements for entrance into His temples. We become unjust stewards and doorkeepers if we add to, alter, remove, or water down the questions we have been instructed to ask.

---

[3] see Edward L. Kimball (1998) "The History of LDS Temple Admission Standards" *Journal of Mormon History* 24: 135-176.

- What can we learn from each response, which is a simple "yes or no" (yea or nay) as mentioned in the Sermon on the Mount? Listen to the Spirit to see if there is anything further that needs to be explored
- On the final question, assessing their worthiness some members struggle; responses on the previous questions should provide confidence in responding to the last one
- When we use the interview process as a teaching moment, those we visit with will be blessed and we will be edified as well; I can testify that revelation has come to me as I have used the precious time I have with members of our stake to teach a few small and simple things regarding the Gospel of Jesus Christ
- We and the members we meet with are blessed when we take an opportunity to express gratitude for their worthiness and commitment to live the Gospel of Jesus Christ

In a January 2003 leadership training meeting, then Elder Henry B. Eyring of the Quorum of the Twelve Apostles spoke on "Standards of Worthiness." I was serving as a bishop at the time and still have my notes from this talk, which impacted my perspective on temple recommend interviews more than any other talk I have heard before or since. May I share one section from this talk that was particularly powerful to me:

"The Lord's standard of worthiness includes some commandments we cannot break. We must be chaste. We must be full-tithe payers. We must keep the Word of Wisdom. We must be honest. And those commandments must be kept with faith in the Lord Jesus Christ and with a humble and repentant heart. Because we love the people we serve, all of us want to do better in lifting our Heavenly Father's children to the faithfulness and purity they need, to have all the blessings of the Lord. Brethren, my purpose today is to help you find ways to do that. ... Lifting people to [the standard the Lord has set to receive a temple recommend] is a great test of our leadership. The standard is very high. It has to be. Those who meet it are worthy to enter the house of the Lord. They have to be pure enough to go where the Lord Himself can go."

I wrote the following poem, *In His Holy Temple*, in 2014:

Dressed in radiant white
And filled with His glorious light
I will serve Him day and night
With all my heart, mind, strength, and might
In His Holy Temple

I seek Him – and He answers
I obtain peace and rest to my soul
Windows of heaven open to me
As I learn and become all that I am meant to be
In His Holy Temple

With my ancestors encouraging and drawing nigh
I can be endowed with power from on high
He blesses, teaches, strengthens, inspires
And I grow in faith, hope, charity and desires
In His Holy Temple

Truly blessings await and eternal rewards are in store
All I am asked to do is to approach the temple door
Clean from the filth of this world and striving to be pure from sin
So that He with open arms can welcome me in!
Into His Holy Temple

Getting our members into His Holy Temple will bring great
blessings to our families, our wards, and our stake. It is worth every
sacrifice to be up and doing this effort.

Chapter 5

The Kirtland Temple and the Gathering of Israel

"Moses appeared…and committed…the keys of the gathering of Israel"
– D&C 110:11

President Nelson has invited us to be up and doing in gathering Israel on both sides of the veil. The keys to the gathering of Israel in this dispensation were restored to the earth in Kirtland, Ohio in 1836. On June 22, 2019, our stake youth, young single adults, and their leaders gathered for a special meeting in the Kirtland Temple. I conducted the meeting and these are the words I shared.

Our stake youth committee selected "Turning Hearts" as a theme for this year's youth conference. In this very room is where the Old Testament prophet Elijah came on April 3, 1836 to restore priesthood keys that would enable the turning of hearts of people to their ancestors. Thus, family history and temple work for our dispensation began here – in this very room.

I am grateful to the Community of Christ, formerly known as the Reorganized Church of Jesus Christ of Latter Day Saints until 2001, for taking good care of this wonderful building and for allowing us to meet here today.

I am grateful to be here in the Kirtland Temple with Brother and Sister DeWeese – Moses and Zipporah – and with all of you who have symbolically been organized into the Twelve Tribes of Israel, which have now grown to 14 tribes plus the young single adults from our stake. Truly we are experiencing the gathering of Israel today! Many, many people have worked to bring this youth conference together and I am thankful for their efforts. I hope that each of you will take the time to thank your Ma & Pa and other stake leaders who represent the Tribe of Levi in their role of helping bring you to the temple today.

Endowment of Power

This is where the ability to gather Israel began. I want to share with you today why the Kirtland Temple matters to me and why it should matter to you.

The Prophet Joseph Smith taught: "What was the object of gathering...the people of God in any age of the world? ... The main object was to build unto the Lord a house whereby He could reveal unto His people the ordinances of His house and the glories of His kingdom and teach the people the way of salvation. ... It is for the same purpose that God gathers together His people in the last days, to build unto the Lord a house to prepare them for the ordinances and endowments, washings and anointings" (*History of the Church*, 5:423-424).

At a general conference of the Church held in January 1831, Joseph Smith received a revelation which commanded the Church to go to Ohio where they would receive the law of the Lord and "be endowed with power from on high" (see D&C 38:32). The law of the Lord came one week after Joseph arrived in Kirtland and is now recorded in D&C 42. We might think of this section today as a Church handbook of instructions. In D&C 42, the Lord also foreshadowed His visit to the Kirtland Temple stating: "I shall come to my temple" (D&C 42:36). But, the visit of the Lord to His temple and the promised endowment of power took another five years to receive because this temple had to be built first.

Building the Temple

A revelation received in December 1832 requested the members of the Church to "establish a house, even a house of prayer, a house of fasting, a house of faith, a house of learning, a house of glory, a house of order, a house of God" (D&C 88:119).

But since Joseph Smith and the other early members of the Church had never seen a temple before, how would they know what to build? The First Presidency of the Church – Joseph Smith, Sidney Rigdon, and Frederick G. Williams – were shown the temple in vision as promised in D&C 95:14 "Therefore, let it be built after the manner which I shall show unto three of you." They were shown the plans for the temple much like a virtual reality video game. Frederick G. Williams recounted the experience this way: "We went upon our knees, called on the Lord, and the Building appeared within viewing distance. I being the first to discover it. Then all of us viewed it together. After we had a good look at the exterior, the Building seemed to come right over us, and the Makeup on this Hall seemed to coincide with what I there saw [in vision] to [the smallest detail]" (from Truman O. Angell's record of FGW's narrative quoted in *The Savior in Kirtland*, p. 211).

Building this temple was no picnic. Members of the Church were poor, and Satan did everything he could to stop construction on this temple. The cornerstone of the Kirtland Temple was laid on July 23, 1833. That very same day members of the Church were driven from their homes in Jackson County, Missouri, by mobs that burned the printing press in Independence. This was no coincidence. Brigham Young later stated that "we never began to build a temple without the bells of hell beginning to ring" (*Discourses of Brigham Young*, p. 410).

The *History of the Church* records in January 1834: "The threats of mobs about Kirtland through the fall and winter had been such as to cause the brethren to be constantly on the lookout, and those who labored on the temple were engaged at night watching to protect the walls they had laid during the day, from threatened violence" (*History of the Church* 2:2).

But those working on the temple got some extra help. A member named Roger Orton shared that he "saw a mighty angel riding upon a horse of fire, with a flaming sword in his hand, followed by five others, encircle the [temple], and protect the Saints…" (*Joseph Smith Papers* J1:174).

Finally, at the end of 1835 the temple was completed enough to start meeting in it. Many experiences occurred that demonstrated that here was truly a house of learning and a house of glory.

Visions and Blessings

During the winter months of early 1836 while the interior of the temple was still being finished, a school of the elders was held. Many visions and blessings were received. In January 1836, the Prophet Joseph Smith received a revelation about the Celestial Kingdom as recorded now in D&C 137. The experiences that William W. Phelps shared with the other church leaders who received their endowment of power served as the source of inspiration for the words found in "The Spirit of God Like a Fire Is Burning."

Temple Dedication and the Following Week

The Kirtland Temple dedication took place on Sunday, March 27, 1836. Almost a thousand people crowded into this room for a 7-hour meeting that ran from 9AM to 4PM. Many people had to be turned away. A second dedicatory service was held four days later for those who could not get in on March 27.

Seated in the top pulpit behind me was President Frederick G. Williams, Joseph Smith, Senior, and W.W. Phelps. The next row down had President Sidney Rigdon, the Prophet Joseph Smith, and his brother Hyrum Smith. Seated below them was David Whitmer, Oliver Cowdery, and John Whitmer. The pulpits on the east side of the room were for the Aaronic Priesthood leaders including the Bishop of Kirtland, Newell K. Whitney, and his counselors and the Bishop in Missouri, Edward Partridge, and his counselors. There were heavenly visitors as well. Frederick G. Williams reported that an angel came through the window during the opening prayer and sat down between him and Father Smith. This heavenly being remained there during the prayer. (You have to wonder how he knew this unless he opened his eyes and peeked.)

The meeting consisted of singing and speaking – much like what we are doing today – only a little longer. Sidney Rigdon spoke for two-and-a-half hours using Matthew 8:20 as his text. "The foxes have holes, and the birds of the air have nests; but the Son of man hath not where to lay his head." His purpose was to point out that now with a temple built, the Savior would no longer be homeless but would have a house to visit here on the earth.

Church officers were sustained in a solemn assembly – meaning that members of each quorum were invited to stand separately with their fellow quorum members and sustain their leaders. This first solemn assembly began the practice that we still have today when a new president of the Church is sustained in General Conference.

Joseph Smith then read a dedicatory prayer that he had written with input from Oliver Cowdery and Sidney Rigdon. This prayer is now found in D&C 109 of our Doctrine & Covenants. Following the dedicatory prayer, the congregation sang "The Spirit of God Like a

Fire Is Burning", which W.W. Phelps had written specifically for the Kirtland Temple dedication. The sacrament was administered, several others spoke, and the meeting concluded with the Hosanna shout, where the words "Hosanna! Hosanna! Hosanna to God and the Lamb, Amen, Amen, and Amen!" are repeated three times. This practice is still done today in temple dedications.

There was a great outpouring of the Spirit and a number of people saw visions, prophesied, or spoke in tongues. Throughout the week following the temple dedication, other meetings were held where heavenly manifestations occurred. On Wednesday, March 30, 1836, about 300 church leaders gathered in the temple and received the ordinance of washing of feet – and an endowment of power.

The highlight of this dedicatory week occurred the following Sunday, April 3, 1836. In this very room, our Lord and Savior Jesus Christ came to accept this dedicated House of the Lord as His own. In the afternoon, following another church meeting attended by almost a thousand people, Joseph Smith and Oliver Cowdery went up to the next to the top row of these pulpits and lowered a heavy canvas curtain, which they called "the veil of the temple." This enabled them to pray in private. What occurred next is recorded in D&C 110…

When D&C 110 Became Meaningful to Me

Thirty years ago, as a young missionary in Massachusetts, I had the opportunity to teach a Christian outreach minister named Maurice Caron in small town north of Boston. He was the most interesting person I taught my entire mission – and probably the most knowledgeable in the Bible. My companion, Elder Craig Petrie, and I had met him on the street in May 1989, and he had invited us to his home to discuss the Bible and the Book of Mormon. In those days we had six discussions that we would teach, and Maurice agreed to listen to our message. I think perhaps he thought he could convert us to become members of his church if we talked long enough. Our visits were pleasant though, and we enjoyed feeling the Spirit together that summer as we discussed truths contained in the scriptures.

It was during our third discussion with Maurice that I came to appreciate the blessings of the Restored Gospel of Jesus Christ in a new way. My eyes were opened, and my heart was forever changed by the experience. I think it was the first time in my life that I realized that we have wonderful knowledge in the Church of Jesus Christ of Latter-day Saints that we often fail to appreciate. And it had everything to do with what happened here in the Kirtland Temple.

My companion and I taught how the Aaronic and Melchizedek Priesthood power were restored to Joseph Smith and Oliver Cowdery in 1829 by John the Baptist and by Peter, James, and John. When Maurice asked why Peter, James, and John came to restore priesthood power and how they had gotten the Melchizedek Priesthood, I invited him to turn to Matthew 17 in the New Testament. We opened our Bibles and read the experience these early Apostles had with Jesus Christ, Moses, and Elijah on the Mount of Transfiguration.

When we finished reading, Maurice shared that he did not understand what was going on in these verses of scripture. I was amazed. Here was a minister who had spent many years studying the Bible – and I, a 20-year old kid, knew something he didn't. And all I had had to do was pay attention in my early morning seminary class – and have some knowledge of the Doctrine & Covenants!

D&C 110 and Matthew 17 Connected

My companion and I introduced Maurice to the Doctrine &
Covenants. After explaining that it contained revelations received
about 150 years earlier by the Prophet Joseph Smith, we read with
him all of the verses in D&C 110. Those of you who were in
seminary this past year (and if you were not sleeping that morning)
may recall that D&C 110 was written by the Prophet Joseph Smith
after a series of visions and visitations took place in this very room
in the Kirtland Temple on April 3, 1836. He recorded the
experience of that day in his journal and this record became D&C
110.

Listen carefully as I share the words that Joseph Smith recorded
from his experience that day. An experience that took place on the
top pulpit above me with a large curtain hanging around it.

The heading for D&C 110 states: *Visions manifested to Joseph Smith the
Prophet and Oliver Cowdery in the temple at Kirtland, Ohio, April 3, 1836.
The occasion was that of a Sabbath day meeting. Joseph Smith's history states:
"In the afternoon, I assisted the other Presidents in distributing the Lord's
Supper to the Church, receiving it from the Twelve, whose privilege it was to
officiate at the sacred desk this day. After having performed this service to my
brethren, I retired to the pulpit, the veils being dropped, and bowed myself, with
Oliver Cowdery, in solemn and silent prayer. After rising from prayer, the
following vision was opened to both of us."*

1 The veil was taken from our minds, and the eyes of our understanding
were opened.
2 We saw the Lord standing upon the breastwork of the pulpit, before us;
and under his feet was a paved work of pure gold, in color like amber.
3 His eyes were as a flame of fire; the hair of his head was white like the
pure snow; his countenance shone above the brightness of the sun; and

his voice was as the sound of the rushing of great waters, even the voice
of Jehovah, saying:

4 I am the first and the last; I am he who liveth, I am he who was slain; I
am your advocate with the Father.

5 Behold, your sins are forgiven you; you are clean before me; therefore,
lift up your heads and rejoice.

6 Let the hearts of your brethren rejoice, and let the hearts of all my
people rejoice, who have, with their might, built this house to my name.

7 For behold, I have accepted this house, and my name shall be here; and
I will manifest myself to my people in mercy in this house.

8 Yea, I will appear unto my servants, and speak unto them with mine
own voice, if my people will keep my commandments, and do
not pollute this holy house.

9 Yea the hearts of thousands and tens of thousands shall greatly rejoice
in consequence of the blessings which shall be poured out, and
the endowment with which my servants have been endowed in this house.

10 And the fame of this house shall spread to foreign lands; and this is the
beginning of the blessing which shall be poured out upon the heads of my
people. Even so. Amen.

11 After this vision closed, the heavens were again opened unto us;
and Moses appeared before us, and committed unto us the keys of
the gathering of Israel from the four parts of the earth, and the leading of
the ten tribes from the land of the north.

12 After this, Elias appeared, and committed the dispensation of
the gospel of Abraham, saying that in us and our seed all generations after
us should be blessed.

13 After this vision had closed, another great and glorious vision burst
upon us; for Elijah the prophet, who was taken to heaven without tasting
death, stood before us, and said:

14 Behold, the time has fully come, which was spoken of by the mouth of
Malachi—testifying that he [Elijah] should be sent, before the great and
dreadful day of the Lord come—

15 To turn the hearts of the fathers to the children, and the children to
the fathers, lest the whole earth be smitten with a curse—

16 Therefore, the keys of this dispensation are committed into your
hands; and by this ye may know that the great and dreadful day of the
Lord is near, even at the doors.

Now with the context and understanding that comes from the
Restored Gospel of Jesus Christ and a modern prophet, listen to
the words from Matthew 17:1-11 read from the same Bible that I
read with Maurice that day – and with some commentary based on
what the Spirit taught me that day in Maurice's home and what I
have learned in my scripture study since then:

1 And after six days Jesus taketh Peter, James, and John his brother, and
bringeth them up into an high mountain apart, *[Jesus is taking these three
Apostles – His future First Presidency – to the temple to teach them and to give them
priesthood keys; whenever you see the phrase "into a mountain" in the scriptures, it is
referring to a temple experience]*
2 And was transfigured before them: and his face did shine as the sun, and
his raiment was white as the light. *[Jesus is described in much the same way that
Joseph Smith described Him in D&C 110 as glowing]*
3 And, behold, there appeared unto them Moses and Elias talking with
him. *[Note that the footnote says that Elias is the prophet Elijah in this instance.
Moses and Elijah, who were both translated and therefore never died, would have their
physical bodies before the resurrection of Jesus so that they could lay their hands on the
apostles' heads to bestow on them priesthood keys]*
4 Then answered Peter, and said unto Jesus, Lord, it is good for us to be
here: if thou wilt, let us make here three tabernacles; one for thee, and one
for Moses, and one for Elias.
5 While he yet spake, behold, a bright cloud overshadowed them: and
behold a voice out of the cloud, which said, This is my beloved Son, in
whom I am well pleased; hear ye him. *[Heavenly Father provides His witness
that Jesus was His Son]*
6 And when the disciples heard *it,* they fell on their face, and were
sore afraid.
7 And Jesus came and touched them, and said, Arise, and be not afraid.
8 And when they had lifted up their eyes, they saw no man, save Jesus
only.

9 And as they came down from the mountain, Jesus charged them, saying,
Tell the vision to no man, until the Son of man be risen again from
the dead.
10 And his disciples asked him, saying, Why then say the scribes that Elias
must first come?
11 And Jesus answered and said unto them, Elias truly shall first come,
and restore all things.

Yes, Elias, Moses, and Elijah have come! And in this very room,
they restored priesthood keys that enable the blessings of the
Gospel of Jesus Christ to go forth to the world. The ability to
Proclaim the Gospel (restored by Moses), to Perfect the Saints
(restored by Elias), and to Redeem the Dead (restored by Elijah)
began here – in this very room.

In teaching Maurice that day 30 years ago, I came to realize that as
members of the Restored Church of Jesus Christ we have additional
scripture and knowledge that help us understand the Bible better.
What a wonderful blessing! I hope that you can each come to
appreciate that blessing for yourself.

The Significance of April 3, 1836

D&C Section 110 records that after our Savior Jesus Christ
appeared and accepted the Kirtland Temple as His house, three
additional visitors came in separate visions: first Moses, then Elias,
and finally Elijah. All of the keys received that special day relate to
different aspects of the gathering of Israel in preparation for the
Second Coming of the Lord Jesus Christ.

The keys received from Moses enable members and missionaries
alike to proclaim the gospel with authority. The priesthood keys
received from Elias help in the mission of perfecting the Saints as
we strengthen home and family. Celestial marriage, eternal families,
and all of the blessings of Abraham, Isaac, and Jacob flow from the
Abrahamic covenant that Elias renewed. The priesthood keys

received from Elijah enable worthy members today to redeem the dead, perform temple ordinances, and unite family members who have passed beyond the veil.

Moses restored the keys of the gathering of Israel on Sunday, April 3, 1836. This day was unusual because it was both Easter and Passover – and a day in which the heavens were aligned in the very same way they had been aligned on April 3, 33 A.D., the day that Jesus arose from the grave (see *The Lord's Holy Days: Powerful Witnesses of Truth*, p. 60). An article published in the July 1985 *Ensign* by astronomer John Pratt notes the significance of April 3, 1836: "From an astronomer's point of view, this is no small coincidence. This result seems to clearly support the conclusion that it was not a matter of chance that Elijah's return occurred on an Easter Sunday [fitting exactly the one] of the Resurrection."[4]

The Gathering of Israel in Our Dispensation

We are gathered here today representing the twelve tribes of Israel: Reuben, Simeon, Judah, Ephraim, Manasseh, Benjamin, Issachar, Zebulun, Dan, Asher, Gad, and Naphtali. The stake leaders represent the Tribe of Levi who helped get you to the temple today, as they did anciently.

Will we do our part in gathering Israel on both sides of the veil? Hopefully the experience you are having in this very room will strengthen you in going forward with faith and courage. Will your heart be turned by what you have heard and felt today?

---

[4] https://www.churchofjesuschrist.org/study/ensign/1985/07/the-restoration-of-priesthood-keys-on-easter-1836-part-2-symbolism-of-passover-and-of-elijahs-return?lang=eng

My Personal Witness

I would like to conclude with a few comments on the songs and speakers that will follow me. The next song that the choir will sing is important to me personally because the version of "Come Thou Fount of Every Blessing" that will be sung was arranged by one of my missionary companions, Craig Petrie. Elder Petrie and I were the ones who taught the minister that I told you about earlier when we served together in Lawrence, Massachusetts 30 years ago.

Our next speaker, Sherilyn Farnes, grew up in our stake. My wife was her young woman leader almost 25 years ago. Sherilyn has gone on to become an expert in Church history and we are delighted that she has agreed to join us today to share some of her thoughts on helping write the new Church history book *Saints*.

I leave you with my testimony that Jesus Christ is our Savior. He loves us dearly and completed His Atonement for us so that we can return home to our Heavenly Parents. The experiences that happened here in this very room more than 183 years ago were real. We are in the same sacred space that our Savior Jesus Christ and His prophets Moses, Elias, and Elijah came to restore priesthood keys on Easter Sunday, April 3, 1836. I testify that those priesthood keys are held today by a living prophet President Russell M. Nelson. Those same priesthood keys – to proclaim the Gospel and gather scattered Israel, to perfect the Saints, and to redeem the dead – are active in the Seneca Maryland Stake and held by President Darren Arnold. I look forward to the message that he has to share with us. I know that President Arnold has been called of God to lead our stake at this time. And I am grateful that I have the chance to be with you here today to listen to his inspired message.

In the name of Jesus Christ, amen.

Chapter 6

The Doctrine of Returning and Reporting

"When performance is measured, performance improves. When performance is measured and reported, the rate of improvement accelerates."
- President Thomas S. Monson

Follow-up with our leaders comes after ministering to others and being up and doing. We complete delegated assignments by returning and reporting. This talk was given in a stake priesthood leadership meeting held March 21, 2021. Portions of this message were also shared in a June 2018 leadership meeting.

I invite you to take notes, take time to ponder what you learn from what is spoken or spiritually discerned, and most importantly take action with those impressions. Or more simply put – hear Him and follow Him!

Messages from This Week's *Come, Follow Me*

I have learned so much since the beginning of this year in studying the Doctrine & Covenants and Church history. Emma & Joseph Smith, Martin Harris, Oliver Cowdery, and a host of other early members of the Church have all become more real to me as I have sought to understand their lives and challenges. I am thankful for the opportunity that we have to learn, live, and teach the Gospel of Jesus Christ as we participate in *Come, Follow Me.*

This past week we have studied D&C Sections 27 and 28. I invite you to turn to these sections in your scriptures or your Gospel

Library app. Both are relevant to what I feel inspired to discuss this evening in terms of the doctrine of returning and reporting.

President Boyd K. Packer famously taught[5]: "True doctrine, understood, changes attitudes and behavior." So I hope this evening we can come to better understand the true doctrine of returning and reporting – and be able to apply it in our own lives and stewardships.

Doctrines focus on the *why*, **principles** upon the *what*, and **applications** upon the *how*[6]. In our discussions together after my talk, we hope to counsel together on aspects of the how – the application in our lives and priesthood service of returning and reporting. But first we must seek to understand the doctrine and principles – the why and the what – of this important aspect of the Gospel of Jesus Christ.

The Purpose of the Sacrament

D&C Section 27 was received in August 1830 just four months after the Church of Christ was established. I marvel at the power of the message received to a young prophet who is not yet 25 years old! On his way to purchase wine for a sacrament service to precede the confirmation of his wife Emma as a member of the Church, Joseph is met by a heavenly messenger and taught lessons for him and for all of us.

The first four verses of this section discuss the sacrament ordinance that we perform each week. In verse 2, Joseph Smith is taught by a heavenly messenger that *what* we eat and drink as emblems of our Savior's sacrifice as not as important as *why* we do it.

[5] https://www.churchofjesuschrist.org/study/ensign/1986/11/little-children?lang=eng
[6] See Elder Bednar's 2011 book *Increase in Learning*

We partake of the sacrament to remember the great love that our Savior has for each of us personally and to witness our willingness to follow Him "with an eye single to [His] glory." And what is God's glory? Joseph had just received Moses 1:39 two months earlier so he would have been familiar with the passage we know so well as declared by Jehovah, our Savior Jesus Christ: "For behold, this is my work *and my glory* – to bring to pass the immortality and eternal life of man." Or, as President Russell M. Nelson has rephrased this concept, to gather Israel on both sides of the veil. God's glory is the salvation and exaltation of each one of His precious children. And we are invited to participate with Him in this effort.

Preparing to Return and Report at Adam-ondi-Ahman

Then in verse 5 of D&C 27, Joseph Smith is taught "for the hour cometh that I [meaning Jesus Christ] will drink of the fruit of the vine with you [meaning Joseph Smith as the head of this dispensation] on the earth." Our Savior and the Prophet Joseph will be joined in this priesthood meeting with a host of other key holders and leaders noted in verses 5 to 13. These key holders include Moroni, Elias, John the Baptist, Elijah, Joseph of Egypt and his father Jacob, his grandfather Isaac, and his great-grandfather Abraham along with Adam (or Michael), and Peter, James, and John. Thus, representatives of all the dispensations will be present at a special sacrament meeting in the future with Jesus Christ and with the Prophet Joseph Smith. Remember this revelation is received before many of the priesthood keys would be bestowed upon Joseph Smith and Oliver Cowdery in the Kirtland Temple. The events described in D&C 110 would not occur for almost another six years – until April 3, 1836. I marvel to reflect upon how Joseph is learning line upon line just a few months after the Lord's church has been restored to the earth.

Why does this matter to you and to me? Because in verse 14, we read about another important group that will be asked to come to this meeting: "And also with all those whom my Father hath given me out of the world." These individuals are those, women and men, who are on the covenant path, who have made covenants and promises with God at baptism and in holy temples. These are you and me. We, as covenant keepers and as priesthood leaders, will be invited to participate in this future priesthood and sacrament meeting – a meeting to be held in Western Missouri at a place called Adam-ondi-Ahman.

I grew up in the Liberty, Missouri Stake and this sacred site was a place that my family and I visited when I was a teenager. During the 1980s, we watched in wonder as many senior couples and service missionaries were called to beautify this site. I, along with other youth in our stake, went to Adam-ondi-Ahman for seminary activities and youth conferences to pick up rocks and sticks and to help in a little way to prepare this land for the Second Coming of our Savior. I can recall thinking at the time – this seems like the same rock I picked up last year! Are we making any progress here?

Each time I return to Missouri for a high school reunion I visit this sacred site. Some of my most significant spiritual experiences have occurred as I have pondered and prayed in a beautiful grove of trees in Adam-ondi-Ahman.

Today this site is much prettier than it was forty years ago. And it will be even more beautiful when it is graced as Isaiah recorded[7] (and Abinadi later teaches in the Book of Mormon[8]) by "the feet of Him that bringeth good tidings, that published peace, that bringeth good tidings of good, that published salvation; that saith unto Zion, Thy God reigneth!"

---

[7] Isaiah 52:7-10
[8] Mosiah 12:21-24

In his book *The Millennial Messiah*, Elder Bruce R. McConkie of the Quorum of the Twelve Apostles wrote the following: "… as all the spirits of men attended the grand council in preexistence, so all the righteous shall attend a like council at Adam-ondi-Ahman before the winding-up scenes" (p. 583). "Those who have held keys and powers and authorities in all ages from Adam to the present will be also be present…It will be the greatest congregation of faithful saints ever assembled on planet earth" (p. 579). "Every prophet, apostle, president, bishop, elder, or church officer of whatever degree – **all who have held keys shall stand before him who holds all the keys. They will then be called upon to give an account of their stewardships and to report how and in what manner they have used their priesthood and their keys for the salvation of men within the sphere of their appointments**" (p. 582).

How did the Church in this dispensation first learn about this return and report event and special priesthood and sacrament meeting at Adam-ondi-Ahman that will precede the Second Coming of Jesus Christ to the whole earth? D&C Section 27:4-14 – from this week's *Come, Follow Me!*

Is your priesthood service now in the Seneca Maryland Stake of Zion preparing you for this future meeting to be held at Adam-ondi-Ahman with your Savior Jesus Christ? What will *your* return and report look during that glorious event? That is entirely up to you.

I pray that your priesthood service and my priesthood service now and in the future may qualify us to be as recorded in Isaiah 52:8-10 [with some insertions from me]: "Thy watchman [meaning priesthood leaders in the Seneca Maryland Stake] shall lift up the voice [when they return and report to their Lord and Savior at

Adam-ondi-Ahman]; with the voice together shall they sing: for they shall see eye to eye, when the Lord shall bring again Zion. Break forth into joy, sing together, ye waste places of Jerusalem [even in every ward of the Seneca Maryland Stake]: for the Lord hath comforted his people, he hath redeemed Jerusalem. The Lord hath made bare his holy arm in the eyes of all the nations; and all the ends of the earth shall see the salvation of our God [when He returns for His Second Coming]."

Learning from the Account of the Creation of this Earth

At the time that D&C 27 and 28 were received, Joseph Smith was also studying the Bible and working on the Joseph Smith translation of the book of Genesis. The insights gained during June 1830 to February 1831 led to the book of Moses in *The Pearl of Great Price* – and eventually to lessons taught in the temple endowment.

The patterns used by Heavenly Father and His Son Jesus Christ in creating the earth are instructive in helping us understand how to succeed as priesthood leaders. The temple endowment, which is a gift to us from a loving Father in Heaven, can be used as a lens into this topic. Since this is a leadership meeting, I would like to consider how the endowment models leadership behavior. Doctrines and leadership principles taught in the endowment can help us in our efforts and service as leaders. I believe we can discuss a few of them to gain valuable insights without going into specifics that might be too sacred to discuss outside of the temple.

The Plan of Salvation Began with a Ministering Interview

Consider that the efforts to put the Plan of Salvation into action likely began in a council meeting. We do not have a lot of revealed details on the pre-mortal existence, but **perhaps the Plan of Salvation really began in a ministering interview between**

Elohim and Jehovah, where the Father taught His Son what was needed and invited Him to minister to the rest of their family.

Our Father in Heaven set the vision and our Savior put that vision into effect. Jesus Christ presented the Father's plan in the council meeting that we refer to as "the Council in Heaven" and Jesus agreed to go down and to be our Savior. Following this council meeting, the leaders of the Council in Heaven then "went down" to put the plan into action for our benefit (see Abraham 3:24-25). Likewise, plans to minster to others are not accomplished simply in meetings. We must go down and visit people. Like the sons of Mosiah as recorded in Alma 26:29, we need to "[enter] into their houses and [teach] them." And as we "show forth good examples unto [the people] … [the Lord] will make an instrument of [us] in [His] hands unto the salvation of many souls" (Alma 17:11). His work and His glory is to bring to pass the immortality and eternal life of man (Moses 1:39). Ministering is simply assisting Heavenly Father in His work and His glory through serving others.

The Bible and the Book of Genesis begins with action on the part of God in creating the world without any mention of the planning efforts and vision established by leaders during the Council in Heaven. How grateful I am for the further light and knowledge that we have been blessed with due to modern revelation including the temple endowment and *The Pearl of Great Price*. Perhaps one of the plain and precious things that was removed from the Bible (1 Nephi 13:28) that has caused "an exceedingly great many [to] stumble…that Satan has great power over them" (1 Nephi 13:29) is that **counseling with our councils precedes creation.**

Elder Bruce R. McConkie taught (BYU Speeches, August 15, 1972): "Everyone really has a different personal plan of salvation." Each of us is at a different place on our own journey along the covenant path. We need to assist one another in getting back to our heavenly home. I know that effective ministering interviews coupled with ward councils where specific plans are put into place to assist those in need will enable our ministering efforts and the creation of an environment where we can flourish as brothers and sisters in these latter-days.

Lessons on Ministering and Ministering Interviews from the Temple Endowment

Now let's see if we can have eyes to see some important leadership principles modeled and taught in the temple endowment. If we pay close attention, we can be taught how God the Father (Elohim) delegates the work needed to create this earth and to minister to its inhabitants.

At the beginning of each period in the creation, Elohim speaks to Jehovah and Michael face-to-face and provides details with specific requests and invites them to report back when they are finished with those tasks. Elohim, as the priesthood leader, is in effect holding a ministering interview with a ministering companionship who are going to go down and visit the earth to accomplish things. Information is provided by revelation, line upon line, precept upon precept. New information is given only after the previous tasks have been completed.

We note that as a loving leader our Heavenly Father establishes the vision for the project, cares deeply for its success, but He does not micromanage the work. I have felt the love that Elohim has for me as I have observed how He interacts with His partners in the Creation. As priesthood leaders, do we express our love for those we serve with and those we ask to minister to others?

In the endowment, we see how Jehovah and Michael return and report progress on a regular basis during the creation. The next time you are in the temple study this interaction carefully and think of it in terms of a ministering interview that you might participate in. Jehovah and Michael gain enthusiasm for their work as their leader expresses appreciation for them and gratitude for their efforts at each stage of the project. To them, their work becomes "glorious and beautiful" just as our ministering efforts can become.

In effect, our Father in Heaven is ministering to His sons as He instructs and guides the efforts of their work. Scriptural accounts of the Creation record that He [meaning God the Father] "saw that [their efforts were] good" and He told them so. **Are we complementing others appropriately when they do well and accomplish good?**

After Adam and Eve were cast out of the Garden of Eden, when they were facing adversity and struggles with the challenges of life in the lone and dreary world, Elohim and Jehovah counsel together and decide to send help. Think of that interaction between the Father and the Son depicted in this part of the endowment as an elders quorum presidency discussing the needs of those they have been called to serve. I hope and pray that we can see ministering assignments being made, performed, and followed up on in our wards in a similar fashion as we see modeled in the temple endowment where angelic messengers were assigned and sent from the presence of God to minister to Adam and Eve.

These messengers were sent to observe, to teach, and to strengthen. They were sent to provide further light and knowledge when those they ministered to were ready to receive it. Following each ministering assignment, they (the messengers) report back to their priesthood leader who had given them specific and inspired instructions for what was needed at the time the assignment was given. The angelic ministers listened and sought heaven's help in bringing the appropriate message to meet real needs.

What are some of the things that these ministers did when they visited Adam and Eve? They came as a ministering companionship to the home of those they were asked to visit and greeted and spoke face-to-face with each member of the household. They came knowing the names of each member of the family. They came to observe and to report back challenges that the family was facing. They answered difficult questions with inspired responses. They taught doctrine. When asked, they even advised the family on financial matters and taught that temporal self-reliance involves having "sufficient for our needs."

They taught the importance of keeping covenants and of being on the covenant path. They observed Satan in action and cautioned those they ministered to against following him and the ways of the world. And when requested to do so by their priesthood leader, they cast Satan out with their testimony and their faith in the power of the Atonement of Jesus Christ, which was the same way that Satan was cast out of heaven originally (see Rev. 12:11 "And they overcame [Satan] by the blood of the Lamb, and by the word of their testimony").

They promised to return – and they kept that promise. They brought a bit of heaven into the lone and dreary world – into the home of Adam and Eve. These servants of God helped those they ministered to in their journey along the covenant path back to their heavenly home. I know that we can do the same!

Our Personal Prayers Allow Us to Return and Report Daily to Heavenly Father

There are many examples in the Church of returning and reporting on priesthood assignments. For example, upon returning from full-time missionary service, our wonderful sisters and elders report to the stake high council. Elder Jason Bishop, who just returned from the Michigan Detroit Mission, reported to us this past Thursday evening. The experience was uplifting to me personally. I observed the growth that Elder Bishop experienced in his missionary service. Following his report, I expressed gratitude for his wonderful example, his report, and his safe return home.

In our ministering assignments, we each have the opportunity to return and report on our efforts and progress in ministering interviews to priesthood leaders. But sometimes we may overlook the most important return and report – the one that we have the opportunity to do each day in our personal prayers. Elder Bednar, in his October 2008 General Conference talk "Pray Always", taught that our evening prayers are an opportunity to return and report to our Heavenly Father on our activities and progress each day.

Elder Bednar stated[9]:

> "Meaningful morning prayer is an important element in the spiritual creation of each day—and precedes the temporal creation or the actual execution of the day. Just as the temporal creation was linked to and a continuation of the spiritual creation, so meaningful morning and evening prayers are linked to and are a continuation of each other.

> "At the end of our day, we kneel again and report back to our Father. We review the events of the day and express heartfelt thanks for the blessings and the help we received. We repent and, with the assistance of the Spirit of the Lord, identify ways we can do and become better tomorrow. Thus our evening prayer builds upon and is a continuation of our morning prayer.

---

[9] https://www.churchofjesuschrist.org/study/general-conference/2008/10/pray-always?lang=eng

And our evening prayer also is a preparation for meaningful morning prayer [the following day].

"Morning and evening prayers—and all of the prayers in between—are not unrelated, discrete events; rather, they are linked together each day and across days, weeks, months, and even years. This is in part how we fulfill the scriptural admonition to "pray always" (Luke 21:36; 3 Nephi 18:15, 18; D&C 31:12). Such meaningful prayers are instrumental in obtaining the highest blessings God holds in store for His faithful children."

I invite you to make your personal prayers a daily return and report to your Heavenly Father. I can testify that gaining an appreciation for this approach to prayer – and acting on it – will change your life!

Oliver Cowdery: His Return and His Report

I want to conclude by turning our attention to D&C 28 and related events that occurred later in Church history involving Oliver Cowdery.

In the first 28 sections of the Doctrine & Covenants, there are at least 12 recorded revelations given to or involving Oliver Cowdery. Thus, more than 40% of the revelations we have studied so far this year relate to "the second elder of this church" as Oliver is referred to by the Lord in D&C 20:3.

How much do you know about him? I have learned a lot in the past several months studying two books[10] about his life. Oliver's life and experiences are quite instructive. I have come to love and appreciate Oliver Cowdery in new ways – and have learned about the power of

---

[10] *Oliver Cowdery: Scribe, Elder, Witness* (BYU, 2006) and *Days Never to be Forgotten: Oliver Cowdery* (BYU, 2009)

ministering and perhaps one of the most remarkable returns and
reports of this dispensation.

D&C 28 was received in September 1830 by the Prophet Joseph
Smith for Oliver Cowdery. Verse 1 explains that Oliver "shall be
heard by the church in all things whatsoever [he] shalt teach them
by the Comforter." Oliver was a powerful teacher and preacher of
the Gospel of Jesus Christ.

Consider that in the 18 months prior to D&C 28 being received,
Oliver served as scribe to Joseph when the Book of Mormon was
translated as well as creating a copy of the Book of Mormon text
for the printer. At that point in Church history, probably no one
knew the Book of Mormon as well as Oliver. He had witnessed
incredible experiences as he would later write[11]: "These were days
never to be forgotten – to sit under the sound of a voice dictated by
the inspiration of heaven…[and he continues]…we were in the
presence of an angel, the certainty that we heard the voice of Jesus,
and the truth … as it flowed from a pure personage, dictated by the
will of God, is to me past description…"

Oliver was with Joseph when heavenly messengers bestowed the
priesthood and priesthood keys. Oliver was the first person
baptized[12] by proper authority in this dispensation, was the first
person ordained to the Aaronic Priesthood, and preached the first
sermon after the Church was organized. The mission that he was
called to serve in verse 8 of D&C 28 literally changed the course of
the Church. In 1834, Oliver was called to be the Associate President
of the Church, an office that we no longer have. Oliver set apart the
first members of the Quorum of the Twelve Apostles in February

---

[11] see footnote to Joseph Smith History 1:71
[12] see Joseph Smith-History 1:71

1835 and gave them their charge[13]. In the Kirtland Temple in April 1836, Oliver with Joseph saw our Savior Jesus Christ and received priesthood keys from Moses, Elias, and Elijah as recorded in D&C 110.

And yet, eight years after the Church was organized, Oliver Cowdery left. In April 1838, the high council in Far West, Missouri excommunicated him. Seeds of pride and contention that are hinted at in D&C 28 bloomed – and Oliver parted ways with the Prophet Joseph. Oliver left Missouri a few months later and moved to Ohio where he went into the practice of law with his brother Lyman. Over the next ten years Oliver and his family lived in small towns in Ohio and Wisconsin[14].

Oliver never knew Nauvoo and the temple endowment restored there. According to one of his law clerks, Oliver learned of the martyrdom of the Prophet Joseph Smith and his brother Hyrum in June 1844 by reading about it in a local newspaper. In 1841, Hyrum Smith had been called as Associate President to replace Oliver as recorded in D&C 124:95-96. I wonder if Oliver thought that it should have been him rather than Hyrum that sealed his mission with his blood alongside Joseph in Carthage.

On October 21, 1848, near Council Bluffs, Iowa, Oliver Cowdery returned to the Church. As Oliver walked into a Church meeting being held outside in a grove of trees there in Iowa, the presiding officer, Elder Orson Hyde of the Quorum of the Twelve Apostles, recognized him, stopped speaking, and immediately came down off the stand to give Oliver a hug. Taking him by the arm, Elder Hyde brought Oliver up onto the stand and after a brief introduction, asked him to speak to the conference.

---

[13] See *History of the Church* 2:194-198
[14] Recently records from his legal cases have been located – a total of 138 cases spanning 1840 to 1848.

Oliver then offered his witness and testimony of the Restoration as his report to almost two thousand people – by far, the largest audience he had ever addressed. A member of the Church named Reuben Miller recorded the words and witness of Oliver Cowdery upon his return and report. Oliver stated: "I wrote with my own pen the entire Book of Mormon (save a few pages) as it fell from the lips of the Prophet as he translated it by the gift and power of God by means of the Urim and Thummim, or as it is called by that book, holy interpreters. I beheld with my eyes and handled with my hands the gold plates from which it was translated. I also beheld the Interpreters. That book is true. … I wrote it myself as it fell from the lips of the Prophet."

A few weeks later on Sunday, November 12, 1848, apostle Orson Hyde re-baptized Oliver Cowdery and re-ordained him an elder in the Melchezidek Priesthood. Following his return Oliver Cowdery stated[15]: "I feel that I can honorably return. I have sustained an honorable character before the world during my absence from you, this [though] a small matter with you, it is of vast importance [to me]. I have ever had the honor of the Kingdom in view, and men are to be judged by the testimony given."

Oliver and his family planned to go to the Salt Lake Valley the following year. However, before taking the journey west, they went to visit his wife's family in Missouri. Sadly, Oliver became sick while there and died in March 1850 at the age of 43.

Impact of Ministering

Oliver Cowdery's return came because of diligent ministering. This ministering was performed by his devoted friend and ministering brother-in-law, Phineas Young. Phineas, the older brother of

---

[15] Quote listed in *Days Never to Be Forgotten*, p. 305

Brigham Young, married Oliver's sister Lucy Cowdery – so there was a family connection between them. Phineas regularly wrote Oliver letters and went out of his way anytime he was in the area to visit Oliver and his family in person. Phineas served as the go between in maintaining contact between Church leaders and Oliver Cowdery.

Phineas never gave up on Oliver – he ministered to him throughout Oliver's 10 years away from the Church! Each time Phineas went East on a mission, he always spent time with Oliver and his family in their home.

Oliver died with his ministering brother by his side. Phineas Young reported that Oliver Cowdery powerfully bore his testimony of the Book of Mormon before passing through the veil. Thus, Oliver concluded his life while fulfilling the last verse in D&C 28: "And thou must open thy mouth at all times, declaring my gospel with the sound of rejoicing."

I add my witness of the truthfulness of the Book of Mormon and of the revelations received in the Doctrine & Covenants. We are blessed to hold the priesthood of God, and we will be called upon to return and report on our service and stewardship.

Chapter 7

Learning in the Light
of the Restoration

"they had been taught by their mothers, that…God would deliver them"
– Alma 56:47

To be up and doing, you must be constantly learning. Who do you learn from and what have you learned? This message was shared in a stake high priest quorum meeting in September 2020.

In preparation for this meeting and for General Conference next week, we have invited all of you to study the Restoration Proclamation that President Nelson shared at our April 2020 conference. I have enjoyed the opportunity to do this. I have marked up a copy, written notes in the margins, and begun working on memorizing it.

I have felt impressed to speak on the topic of "Learning in the Light of the Restoration." As high priests who lead this stake, we must be diligent in our gospel learning and gospel teaching.

I would like to invite you to reflect for a moment about the individual who has had the biggest impact on you personally in learning about the Restoration of the Gospel of Jesus Christ. It might be your father or your mother, a full-time missionary companion, a bishop or other youth leader, a seminary or institute teacher, or a Church leader speaking in General Conference.

For many people, like the 2,060 stripling warriors that Helaman describes in the Book of Mormon, it is the teaching of their mothers that has led to the initial seed of their testimonies of the Restoration. The prophet Helaman shared in a letter to Captain Moroni that these fine young men "had been taught by their mothers, that if they did not doubt, God would deliver them" (Alma 56:47). He then shared the impact of this teaching: "those [young men] were firm and undaunted...they did obey and observe to perform every word of command with exactness..." (Alma 57:20-21). They were covenant makers and covenant keepers because of their mothers.

Today I want to pay tribute to my mother. By word and by example, she influenced me to learn in the light of the Restoration. I have been reading my mother's personal history over the past few weeks. I have been inspired as I have gained a greater appreciation for her background and her influence on our family.

My mother is a pioneer in her family. She grew up in Pittsburgh, Pennsylvania as an only child. Her parents were strict and not particularly religious. They occasionally attended Lutheran, Presbyterian, or Methodist congregations. This lack of religious upbringing did not deter my mother. She had a "thinking log" in the woods near her home where she would sit as a youth and ponder the purpose of life. She records in the preface to her personal history: "In my teenage years, answers were not immediately forthcoming, but I'm certain my experiences prepared the way that when I heard the truth of our existence I was able to recognize and accept it. When I learned there is purpose to life and became a member of The Church of Jesus Christ of Latter-day Saints, I received knowledge and answers I had for so long sought."

My mom joined the Church in 1967 a few weeks after she married my father. Her parents disowned her for joining the Church. I was born about two years later – the first of my parent's seven children.

We grew up not knowing our maternal grandparents. My mom was a pioneer – and pioneers sometimes have to do hard things.

Two years ago my wife and I joined my parents along with several other siblings and their spouses in the Mesa Arizona Temple where we celebrated my mom and dad's 50th temple sealing anniversary.

My mother's legacy is eternal. She rose above her upbringing. All seven of her children are college graduates. And even more important to her, me and my six siblings are sealed to our spouses and faithful members of the Church. Her 30 grandchildren are helping to gather Israel *on this side of the veil* with two currently serving full-time missions and four that have already served.

As the first member of the Church in her direct line, my mom has been motivated to research her family history. Reading her personal history, I have learned of her devoted efforts. She has done temple work for hundreds of her ancestors. She inspires me with efforts to gather Israel and seal eternal families *on the other side of the veil.*

Both my mother and my father love the scriptures and study them diligently. I am a witness of their daily, diligent study – and I am a product of the home they created by being disciples of our Savior Jesus Christ. Their faithful examples have carried over to the next generation, and we are trying to raise our children in the light of the Restoration as she raised me and my six siblings. At age 76, my dear mother teaches early morning seminary and seeks to instill her love for the scriptures to her only student, my niece and her granddaughter Caroline. Such is the power of learning in the light of the Restoration.

At this past April General Conference, President Nelson shared the Restoration Proclamation with the world. In introducing the text, he stated: "We felt impressed to establish a monument of words – words of solemn and sacred proclamation, written not to be carved in tables of stone but in words that could be etched in the fleshy tables of all human hearts."

Have these truths been etched in your heart? What have you learned as you have pondered the truths contained in this Restoration Proclamation?

In my study of the Restoration Proclamation, I have found 20 principles or revealed truths that have been meaningful to me:

1) God loves His children – all of them in every nation of the world
2) By the power of the Father, Jesus rose again
3) Jesus Christ is our Savior, our Exemplar, and our Redeemer
4) Joseph Smith had questions (as a youth)
5) Joseph sought to know and trusted that God would direct him
6) The First Vision started "the restitution of all things"
7) Joseph was instrumental in restoring Christ's Church
8) Heavenly messengers came to instruct and to restore authority
9) The authority to join families together forever has been restored
10) The Book of Mormon was translated by the gift and power of God
11) The Book of Mormon teaches life's purpose and the doctrine of Christ
12) God has a divine plan for our lives
13) Jesus Christ speaks today (will we hear Him?)
14) The Church of Jesus Christ of Latter-day Saints is Christ's New Testament Church restored
15) Jesus Christ has once again called Apostles and has given them priesthood authority
16) Jesus invites all of us to come unto Him…to gain enduring joy
17) The Restoration goes forward through continuing revelation
18) The heavens are open (this we can know!)
19) God is making known His will for His beloved sons and daughters
20) As we prayerfully study the message of the Restoration and act in faith, we will be blessed to gain our own witness

Here are some additional thoughts on several of these principles.

The first revealed truth is found in the first sentence. God loves His children, *all of them*, in every nation of the world. Imagine how different our world would be if everyone appreciated this revealed truth.

Another revealed truth is found in the second paragraph – young Joseph Smith had questions! We need to teach our children and our youth that it is okay to have sincere questions – and that we can trust God to guide us to answers that will help us.

The Restoration Proclamation contains strong verbs: "solemnly proclaim", "declare", "affirm", "witness", "gladly declare", and "testify." It concludes with an invitation to act.

I know as we follow the counsel of our living prophet we will be blessed. I know that the heavens are open because I have personally experienced revelation. I have learned in the light of the Restoration.

I know because I was taught by my mother.

Chapter 8

Our Earthly Apprenticeship:
Learning to Emulate Jesus Christ

"For I have given you an example, that ye should do as I have done to you"
– John 13:15

Who do you follow when you are up and doing? Look for heroes and mentors that can lead you in your life and inspire you to achieve your goals. Our Savior Jesus Christ is our best example and One worth following. This message was given as a sacrament meeting talk in the Derwood Ward on October 21, 2018.

I grew up in Missouri where we had a small horse farm. My father is a farrier, which is a horseshoer and blacksmith – someone who bends metal into a horseshoe and then nails this shoe to the bottom of a horse's foot, so the horse can travel over rocky ground or on paved roads. When I was a teenager, I considered becoming a horseshoer and following my father's profession. I used to swing a big sledge hammer and help my dad make large horseshoes for large draft horses.

My father is a master farrier – and regarded by many as the best in the world in his profession. He has won national and international championships. He has been shoeing horses for over 60 years and written a dozen textbooks used by horseshoeing schools around the world. Today, my dad and my two youngest brothers run a horseshoeing school in northwest Nebraska.

To become a farrier as with many skilled professions, you must serve as an apprentice to a master to learn the skill. You can go to school to learn some of the skills, but it is in the practice as an apprentice that you truly learn and gain the skills you need. An apprentice is a novice, a learner, a working student.

Working as an Apprentice Horseshoer

During the summer after I graduated from high school, I apprenticed with a horseshoer in Kansas City. I worked long, hard, sweaty hours underneath dozens of horses each week. It was hard work, but I learned a lot from this master farrier and teacher. I only came home on the weekends to do laundry and go to church with my family. The rest of the week I gave my heart, might, mind, and strength to learning how to make horseshoes and put them on their feet.

As an apprentice, I closely watched my master and mentor do his work and listened carefully as he taught me each skill I needed to know. Then I would try it. He would correct me if I did something wrong and would encourage me to continue practicing each skill. I learned how to properly lift each of the horse's legs and get safely underneath the horse, how to gently pull the old shoes off, how to trim the horse's foot (which is like trimming a fingernail), how to shape new shoes to fit each of the horse's four feet, and how to carefully nail the shoes onto the horse's feet without hurting them or yourself.

Shoeing horses is backbreaking but rewarding. You are doing something for the horse that the horse cannot do for itself. After weeks of hard work and lots of patience on the part of my teacher, I finally got to the point that I could use the tools properly and do each of the skills necessary to shoe a horse. I wasn't very fast, but I could do the job.

Although I decided to go to college that fall and study chemistry instead of continuing to work with horses' feet, I will always be grateful for those experiences that summer in Kansas City of being an apprentice and learning the skills necessary to be a horseshoer. I can declare like Nephi in the opening verse of the Book of Mormon: "Having been born of goodly parents, therefore I was taught *somewhat* in the learning of my father..." (1 Nephi 1:1; emphasis added).

Coming to Earth to Learn to Become like God

We are spirit children of a loving Father in Heaven and Mother in Heaven. Thus, regardless of our current earthly circumstances each of us possesses a spirit born of goodly parents. We are being invited while on this earth to be taught somewhat in the learning of our Father in Heaven. To help us learn, we have been provided a perfect model of our Father – a Master to which we can apprentice to learn important skills. Our perfect example is our Savior Jesus Christ. As Jesus declared in John 5:19: "The Son can do nothing of himself, but what he seeth the Father do; for what things soever he doeth, these also doeth the Son likewise."

To help us learn, to grow, and to become like Them, our Heavenly Parents prepared a course of instruction for us. We came to earth to gain a body and to learn from our mortal experiences. Thus, we are all apprentices – meaning we are all novices, learners, and working students. Think for a moment about what skills we are trying to learn in this apprenticeship that we call mortal life? What are we apprenticing to become? It is a little more than learning to bend metal and protect horses' feet with sturdy shoes.

Answers to the questions of what we are trying to become are found in the scriptures. From the Old Testament, we are reminded that we are "gods in embryo". Psalms 82:6 states: "Ye are gods; and all of you are children of the most High." From the New Testament, we learn further about our true heritage. The Apostle Paul expressed in Romans 8:16-17: "The Spirit itself beareth witness with our spirit, that we are the children of God. And if children, then heirs; heirs of God, and joint-heirs with Christ."

I would encourage everyone to study the Gospel Topics Essays on LDS.org. These eleven essays are approved by the First Presidency and Quorum of the Twelve Apostles. I know this because a friend of mine wrote the one entitled "Book of Mormon and DNA Studies" with my help. The essay "Becoming Like God" applies to what we are discussing here.

Speaking to assembled Saints in Nauvoo in April 1844, the Prophet Joseph Smith declared: "You have got to learn how to be a god yourself." Wow! Now that is quite the assignment from the Prophet of the Restoration. This vision for why we need to emulate our Savior Jesus Christ. We need to learn to become like Him. We need to acquire His characteristics.

The Gospel Topics Essay on "Becoming Like God" explains that "In order to do [what Joseph Smith invited the people in Nauvoo to do in 1844], the Saints needed to learn godliness, or to be more like God. The process would be ongoing and would require patience, faith, continuing repentance, obedience to the commandments of the gospel, and reliance on Christ. Like ascending a ladder, individuals needed to learn the "first prin[ciples] of the Gospel" and continue beyond the limits of mortal knowledge until they could "learn the last prin[ciples] of the Gospel" when the time came. "It is not all to be comprehended in this world," Joseph said. "It will take a long time after the grave to understand the whole.""

The Prophet Joseph emphasizes that our apprenticeship will take some time and extend beyond this mortal life, so we shouldn't get discouraged. I should point out that in the Church we usually use the term "discipleship" rather than "apprenticeship" but the concept is the same. We seek to follow our Savior Jesus Christ, so we can gain His attributes. The goal is for the apprentice to eventually become like the Master.

How Do We Learn to Become Like God?

How do we learn to become like God? We follow our Savior Jesus Christ. We listen to His chosen leaders and representatives on this earth. We do like the 13th Article of Faith reminds us: "we seek after these things…"

We seek to acquire Christlike attributes. We do this like any apprentice does. We closely watch our Master do His work. We ask questions. We get to work in serving our Savior and our brothers and sisters here on this earth. We listen carefully to the Holy Spirit as He teaches us each skill we need to know. Then we try it. The Spirit will correct us if we do something wrong – this is why we have been given the gift of the Holy Ghost. The Spirit encourages us to continue practicing each skill. We seek to acquire and develop Christlike attributes.

Example with Elder Clark

Usually at one of our stake conferences each year, we have a General Authority or an Area Authority Seventy visit to instruct those who attend these meetings. The stake presidency gets to spend some extra time learning from these visitors. Two years ago, Elder Kim B. Clark of the Seventy visited our stake.

Elder Clark is a master teacher having taught for many years at Harvard Business School before being called first as president of BYU Idaho and then as Commissioner of Church Education, which means that in this role he is in charge of all Church schools and seminary and institute. Those two days he was here for our stake conference I considered myself his apprentice and sought to learn everything I could from him. I served my mission in Boston, which is where Elder Clark is from, so I felt like I had a small connection to him.

His visit came as my first stake conference being a member of the stake presidency, and so I watched Elder Clark very carefully to see what I could learn from him. I noticed that he seemed to be in very good physical condition for someone in his mid-60s. He shared with us that he exercised every day and was careful in his diet. Because I sat next to him on the stand, I could observe Elder Clark very closely during the meetings. I even peeked to see what he was writing during our meetings in a little black book that he had with him. I observed that he was constantly taking notes. When he stood up to speak, he would refer to the notes he had taken and the impressions he had written down, but he had no other prepared remarks.

Based on what I learned from observing Elder Clark, I have sought to emulate or imitate him. I now take notes in every Church meeting I attend. I write impressions I receive – and then I try to act on them. I have changed my daily habits and I now make time to exercise every day. I try to eat heathier so that I can be in better physical condition – like Elder Clark is. As I have sought to emulate Elder Clark in a small way, my life has been blessed. I am much healthier physically and spiritually. I am grateful for this righteous leader, this disciple of Christ, who inspired me to do better in the small and simple things in life so that I can become more like our Savior.

Characteristics of Christ

Disciples emulate (i.e., try to copy) their Master. We must first
know Him and love Him and then do the things He did if we hope
to become like Him. Christ taught in John 13:15 "For I have given
you an example, that ye should do as I have done to you." He
reminds us (John 13:17): "If ye know these things, happy are ye if
ye do them."

What are the characteristics of Christ that we seek to emulate? He
"went about doing good…for God was with him" (Acts 10:38).
D&C 4 and 2 Peter 1 list many of Jesus' attributes: faith, virtue,
knowledge, temperance, patience, brotherly kindness, godliness,
charity, humility, diligence. Preach My Gospel, Chapter 6 reviews
these Christlike attributes and provides a test on page 126 to see
how we are doing.

Follow the Prophet to Learn More about Our Savior

Speaking at the April 2018 General Conference where President
Russell M. Nelson was sustained as the President of the Church of
Jesus Christ of Latter-day Saints, Elder Neil L. Andersen of the
Quorum of the Twelve Apostles shared: "A prophet does not stand
between you and the Savior. Rather, he stands beside you and
points the way to the Savior."

May we follow the prophet in emulating our Savior as we strive to
be up and doing!

Chapter 9

Forming, Storming, Norming, and Performing

"I will go and do the things that the Lord has commanded..."
– 1 Nephi 3:7

When you are up and doing, you must learn to cope with change. Will we have an attitude of "why me?" or one of "send me!"? Change is hard and results in various stages and emotions! The following message was shared during a stake reorganization meeting held September 17, 2017.

We are gathered today to experience a mighty change of a structural nature across our stake. These changes will hopefully lead to mighty changes in each of our personal conversions and commitments to the Gospel of Jesus Christ as we go forward as members of the Seneca Maryland Stake of Zion. Before we get to the details of the ward changes, President Arnold has asked that I take a few minutes to explain the purpose of what we are doing and the doctrine behind why we are doing these reorganizations. I know from experience that understanding the "why" can help us get through any "how" (as discussed in Viktor Frankl's *Man's Search for Meaning*).

Why Reorganize and Change?

So, why are we reorganizing wards across our stake? Simply put – because the Lord wants our very best efforts and we need to prepare for challenges that are coming our way. The scriptures explain that the purpose of a stake is "for a defense, and for a refuge from [storms that are being] poured out … upon the whole earth" (D&C 115:6).

Storms have been in the news a lot lately and more will be coming in these turbulent last days. The spiritual storms that we seek refuge from may in some ways be more impactful on our eternal lives than the hurricanes have been on those struck in Texas and Florida these past few weeks. In short, these ward reorganizations are intended to help us be better prepared for the future.

Member Transfers

This past Monday we had the missionaries over for dinner. Having just learned about the coming changes, one of the elders said enthusiastically, "This coming Sunday will be like missionary transfers – but for all of the members!"

I have reflected this past week on what occurred to me during my missionary transfers while serving in Boston, Massachusetts almost 30 years ago. Some transfers involved me moving to a new city and having to get to know new people and to attend a new church building. Other transfers involved only getting a new companion. In these situations, I had to teach him about our area and introduce him to the members of our ward.

In all cases, each transfer brought new experiences and new growth in my life. Some transfers were harder than others, but each missionary transfer I experienced brought together new capabilities and different personalities that enabled my companion and I as a team to uniquely reach individuals seeking to improve their lives. As a stake presidency, we hope that today's "member transfers" will similarly bring growth in your spiritual lives.

Become a Zion People

Forming or reforming any organization can be a challenge and requires time and patience on the part of all participants. Regular associations at church and the service we provide to one another in our wards create wonderful and lasting friendships. Thus, being asked to attend a different building with new people may feel overwhelming at first. However, new friendships will form as we work together to become a Zion people of one heart and one mind. In Moses 7:18 we are taught that the qualities of a Zion people include being of "one heart" (i.e., being united and caring for others), "one mind" (studying the same topics together), "dwelling in righteousness" (living in families and endeavoring to become better each day), and "having no poor among us" (lifting the burdens of those around us).

Stages of Group Development and Team Building

About 50 years ago, a psychologist named Bruce Tuckman described four stages of group development and team building. These four stages are known as forming, storming, norming, and performing. Sometimes a fifth is added – that of "mourning." We will not focus on that one today – although we recognize that short-term sadness often comes when we experience any change in our surroundings.

I would like to discuss each of these four stages as they relate to our lives in trying to live the Gospel of Jesus Christ. Hopefully these thoughts will help prepare us to go through new experiences in the coming weeks with ward boundary changes that will require forming new groups and building new "teams".

Forming

Forming involves bringing together a group of people to accomplish a common goal. This past week I started a new project team at work. I know from having built teams in the past that beginning a new project is exciting but can be terrifying at the same time. Joining a new ward or welcoming new people into our circle of friends is similar – it can be both exciting and scary at times because it involves change.

In the Church of Jesus Christ of Latter-day Saints, we gather each week in congregations that are defined geographically. These ward boundaries are defined by stake leaders and ultimately approved by the First Presidency.

The Church Handbook of Instructions state (Book 1, Section 9.1.2) that "in the United States and Canada, wards generally should have at least 300 members. All new wards must have at least 15 Melchizedek Priesthood holders who are active in the Church, full-tithe payers, and capable of serving in a priesthood or auxiliary position." As communities of people who serve one another, wards have optimal sizes. If they get too large, they are divided so that people can more effectively serve one another. If wards get too small and there are not enough people to serve in the various callings, then a ward may be dissolved and combined with an adjacent ward or branch so that there are sufficient people available to serve one another.

A ward's size is controlled by its geographic boundaries. The Church Handbook notes that to propose changing a ward boundary, the stake president completes an application form and marks any proposed boundary changes on a map. This completed application is given to an Area Seventy, in our case Elder Calderwood, who reviews the application and if he endorses the proposal, submits it to Church headquarters in Salt Lake City. The Handbook clearly states that "Approval [for a change in ward boundaries] is given only by the First Presidency."

These requirements and detailed process emphasize the importance that the Church places on forming a ward, changing a ward, or discontinuing a ward – because our ward congregations are where the rubber meets the road so to speak in our church lives. Our ward families are important as we live the Gospel of Jesus Christ because they provide an opportunity to serve one another.

Eugene England writes in his book *Why the Church is as True as the Gospel* (p. 6) that two keys to the effectiveness of the church are (1) that it is a lay church with leadership called from its congregations and (2) that those congregations are organized geographically rather than by personal choice. Professor England shares: "The basic Church experience of almost all Mormons brings them directly and constantly into very demanding and intimate relationships with a range of people and problems in their assigned congregations that are not primarily of their own choosing but are profoundly redemptive in potential, in part *because* they are not consciously chosen."

Thus, we do not move to a different ward because we like their bishop better or the demographics of the membership are more appealing to us in some way.

May we be like Ruth in the Old Testament who stated to her mother-in-law Naomi when she was asked to move from Moab to Bethlehem. When essentially being asked to "change wards", Ruth replied "thy people shall be my people, and thy God my God" (Ruth 1:16).

Storming

Storming can occur when emotion impacts our judgment and we get angry or saddened by a situation we encounter. Someone going through a recent ward boundary change in Utah shared on her blog: "Latter-day Saints, like all humans, are very communal creatures and we thrive on stability. We develop a deep family bond with our

congregation members, so the idea of 'breaking up the family' can be an emotional experience."
(https://mormonsoprano.com/2015/02/16/new-boundaries-endings-beginnings/)

I have lived in about a dozen different wards or branches throughout my life. Except for my mission transfers, all previous changes in my church congregations have come due to moves that I chose to make. My family and I have lived in the Gaithersburg 1st Ward for 18 years. We also lived in the Quince Orchard Ward back in the mid-1990s and have many friends there as well. Fifteen years ago, I served as the bishop of the Gaithersburg 1st Ward. I have served with and dearly love hundreds of people who have previously or are currently living in the Gaithersburg 1st Ward. While my current stake calling keeps me from being able to be with my wonderful ward friends every Sunday, my love for them is still very real and meaningful to me.

After our family home evening this past Monday night, my son Ethan said in his closing prayer: "Help us to have a good attitude as we go through these changes to our ward." I am proud of him for recognizing the impact that attitude can have on how we each respond to events in our lives.

The changes that are being presented today will bring a change in the regular contact of members of the current Gaithersburg 1st Ward. My children will no longer be going to church each Sunday with some of their friends. I have imagined their pain and their sorrow even before they knew they would suffer it. Since I have known about these boundary changes for several months, I have faced many emotions already that some of you will be experiencing in the coming weeks. I add my witness that although change is hard, these changes are what are needed to strengthen our members and to ultimately grow our stake.

Norming

Norming is the stage in a group's development when all team members begin to take responsibility and desire to work for the success of the team goals. In the Church of Jesus Christ of Latter-day Saints, I equate this stage to what occurs when we express our support for and sustain our leaders through the law of common consent. In D&C 26:2 we learn: "And all things shall be done by common consent in the church, by much prayer and faith, for all things you shall receive by faith."

In a few minutes, we will each be asked to provide a sustaining vote to the proposal being presented today. What are we doing when we raise our right arms to the square? Are you simply saying "yes" to what is being presented? Are you just agreeing because you think you are supposed to? Or is there more going on in your minds and in your hearts? As we raise our hands in support of the proposed changes today, are we each seeking the Lord's will in our lives and expressing our commitment like Nephi to go and do the things that the Lord has commanded?

I shared with you earlier the prescribed process that is undertaken to reorganize ward boundaries in the Church of Jesus Christ of Latter-day Saints. Boundary changes come about because of a lot of thought and prayer on the part of our stake president and the entire stake presidency and are approved ultimately by the President of the Church and his counselors. Thus, when we raise our hands to sustain the proposed ward boundary changes and the accompanying changes in ward leadership, we are being given an opportunity to sustain our stake president, who had the inspiration to take this action, and the First Presidency who approved the action.

Performing

Performing involves doing our best. Will we use these ward realignments as a spring board to realign our lives to what really matters? Re-booting a computer helps optimize its performance and restores its activity level. As a stake presidency, we hope that this "rebooting of our congregations" can similarly optimize our performance and restore our personal activity levels.

Do we attend Church thinking what is in this for me? Or do we ask, what can I contribute to my ward family? Do we murmur "Why Me?" like Laman and Lemuel who were cut off from their friends in Jerusalem when the Lord through their priesthood leader Lehi asked them to change their ward boundaries first to the Red Sea and then to Bountiful and then to the Promised Land across an ocean? Or do we possess a "Send Me!" attitude like Nephi? Nephi's enthusiasm for following the Lord has made 1 Nephi 3:7 my favorite verse in the Book of Mormon – "I will go and do what the Lord has commanded…" May we always go where the Lord wants us to go, do what He wants us to do, and be what He wants us to be.

Final Thoughts

Forming. Storming. Norming. Performing. Each of us will likely experience these stages of group development as we begin our new wards, which are designed to strengthen our stake members.

President Arnold has felt strongly that the reason we need to realign our ward boundaries is to make our wards more capable of growing. He has a vision of two new wards being formed in the next five years. This level of missionary work will require our very best efforts. Like the allegory of the olive tree related in Jacob 5 in the Book of Mormon, an important purpose of these ward reorganizations is to graft in new branches to our ward families. We are consolidating and focusing strength so that our efforts can be amplified to bless the lives of others.

In Jacob 5, we are asked by the Lord of the vineyard as his servants to "labor diligently with our might" (v. 61) and to "prepare the way" that growth may occur (v. 64). We are reminded in verse 72 that "the Lord of the vineyard labored also with [his servants]." This is the Lord's work and He is actively involved in it – even down to the details of new ward boundaries. This I know.

In a coming day, each of us will "change our ward boundaries" as we complete our time in this second estate and move to the glorious life that will follow this mortal existence. May we be ready to greet our Lord and Savior because of how we responded to temporal and temporary ward boundary changes we experienced here on the 17th day of September in the year of our Lord 2017.

I testify that Jesus is the Christ, our Savior, our Redeemer, and our Friend. His Gospel is the good news! He loves each of us dearly, which is why He gave His life so that we may live again with our Heavenly Father. I am so grateful for the opportunity to re-read the Book of Mormon this year at the invitation of an inspired stake president and a living prophet President Thomas S. Monson. I have received great strength this year as I have read the Book of Mormon with my family at a consistent pace of two pages every day, every day, every day. We will complete the Book of Mormon this coming Friday – on September 22, which is the 190th anniversary of the Prophet Joseph Smith receiving this ancient record from the angel Moroni. I know it is true and will bring us closer to God than any other book!

Chapter 10

The Book of Mormon
and the Value of Scripture Study

"the book shall be of great worth unto the children of men"
– 2 Nephi 28:2

We all face ups and downs in life. Regular scripture study helps sustain us so that we can be up and doing. This message was shared in the adult session of stake conference on December 10, 2016.

Value of the Book of Mormon to Us

We face real challenges in today's world, and we need God's help to get us through these challenges. One way to find that help is by reading, studying, and applying the scriptures.

The Book of Mormon begins with a family – a family with struggles and challenges like what we face. Lehi and Sariah have children who rebel and personal faith that wavers.

The Book of Mormon ends with two righteous believers in Christ who are coping with a degraded society and a dying world. In spite of all they saw and experienced, Mormon and his son Moroni maintain their faith, their hope, and their charity (see Moroni 7).

How did they maintain their righteousness in spite of being awash in a world of evil? **I believe it is because they spent significant time in the scriptures!** They learned many lessons from their study of the scriptural record available to them and passed this information on to us in our day. We are told that they saw our day (Mormon 8:35) and provided stories and lessons so that "[we] may learn to be more wise than [they] have been" (Mormon 9:31). These prophets recorded what we need to know in order to survive our challenging times. Now it is up to us to read and apply this treasured information along with our families.

At the conclusion of his portion of the ancient American record, the prophet Nephi shares in 2 Nephi 28:2 that "the book shall be of great worth unto the children of men." So tonight I ask you to reflect on the question – "what is the Book of Mormon worth to you?" I pray that the Spirit of the Lord may guide my words and touch your hearts so that we may both be "edified and rejoice together" (D&C 50:22).

The Book of Mormon Was Written for Our Day

Regarding the value of the Book of Mormon to us, President Gordon B. Hinckley taught: "Its appeal is as timeless as truth, as universal as mankind. It is the only book that contains within its covers a promise that by divine power the reader may know with certainty of its truth. ... Its narrative is a chronicle of nations long since gone. But in its descriptions of the problems of today's society, it is as current as the morning newspaper and much more definitive, inspired, and inspiring concerning the solutions of those problems. ... My brothers and sisters, without reservation I promise you that if each of you will [read the Book of Mormon], regardless of how many times you previously may have read [it], there will come into your lives and into your homes an added measure of the Spirit of the Lord, a strengthened resolution to walk in obedience to his commandments, and a stronger testimony of the living reality of the Son of God." (General Conference, October 1979)

I consider the Book of Mormon my most cherished possession. Several years ago I purchased a whole box, 50 copies – 15 to give away and 35 for my personal study. I have now read the Book of Mormon more than two dozen times, and I still learn things every time I read. In 2015 and 2016, I studied the topics of humility, patience, and charity – marking a separate copy of the Book of Mormon for each topic.

Levels of Scripture Study

I have found that there are at least three levels of scripture study that impact how tightly we grasp the iron rod on our journey to the tree of life (see John M. Butler, "Making the Scriptures Personal," *Ensign*, Feb. 1999, 70–71). The lowest or "telestial" level is to read out of duty – because we were asked to do so. We are regularly invited by our leaders to read from the Book of Mormon. Doing so will certainly be a blessing in our lives, but if we only do it out of duty, we will miss higher blessings.

The second or "terrestrial" level of scripture study is for knowledge – because we want to learn something from what we read. Under this level of study, we treat the scriptures as a divine textbook and cross-reference verses and read commentaries about the text. Perhaps we find ourselves concentrating more on what had been written *about* the scriptures than the scriptures themselves.

The highest or "celestial" level of scripture study is for application – because we want to become better, because we want to adopt the qualities taught in the scriptures. Under this level of scripture study, we begin reading the scriptures as if we are there experiencing each situation alongside the prophets and the people described (see Brigham Young, *Journal of Discourses* 7:333).

You might ask yourself "How would I respond under similar circumstances and how could these lessons apply to me in my own life?" Perhaps you make notes in the margins of insights from the Spirit. I can testify that the scriptures come alive and take on new meaning as you try to apply them in your life. I know from personal experience that regularly reading the words of scripture and seeking to apply them in your life can bring a spirit that permeates your soul and brings you closer to our Savior Jesus Christ.

Scripture Study Opens the Door to Personal Revelation

To knock on the door of knowledge, direction, comfort or strength, just open the pages of your scriptures or tap the app of your Gospel Library. Jacob 4:6 states: "Wherefore, we search the prophets, and we have many revelations and the spirit of prophecy; and having all these witnesses we obtain a hope, and our faith becometh unshaken."

Jacob teaches us that scripture study – or in his words "search[ing] the prophets – leads to having "many revelations", obtaining hope, and gaining unshaken faith. I would submit that we need these qualities as we face challenging times in these days of "wickedness and vengeance" (Moses 7:60) before the Second Coming. Therefore, we need to be daily searching the prophets – particularly through reading the Book of Mormon.

In an *Ensign* article written in January 1995, Elder Dallin Oaks of the Quorum of the Twelve Apostles explains how the scriptures can lead us to greater light and knowledge. He states: "…the scriptures can be a Urim and Thummim to assist each of us to receive personal revelation. Because we believe that scripture reading can help us receive revelation, we are encouraged to read the scriptures again and again. By this means, we obtain access to what our Heavenly Father would have us know and do in our personal lives today. That is one reason Latter-day Saints believe in daily scripture study."

A Personal Experience of Revelation Received While Reading

My family lives in the Seneca Maryland Stake because of revelation received while reading the Book of Mormon. In 1999, my family and I were living in Menlo Park, California where I worked for a start-up biotech company in the San Francisco Bay Area. I had a long commute and carpooled with a ward member to my job on the other side of the San Francisco Bay. Each morning after arising early I would read the Book of Mormon while eating breakfast. I typically read at a rate of about one to two pages a day. By early March, I was in the middle of the Isaiah chapters of 2 Nephi.

On Monday, March 8, 1999 I was reading in 2 Nephi 19. As I read, I reflected on how the words from the Book of Mormon applied to me and my situation. At this time, my start-up company was not starting up so well because of poor management. We had recently gotten a new CEO, and I was questioning whether or not I should stay with the company. That morning as I read 2 Nephi 19:16 the words took on a very personal meaning and seemed to jump off the page. Nephi was quoting Isaiah, who wrote more than 2700 years ago the following words: "For the leaders of this people cause them to err; and they that are led of them are destroyed."

For me that day I was being told by the Lord to leave my company and take another job to avoid physical, spiritual, and emotional destruction from the leaders of my company. Within a few weeks of reading this passage from the Book of Mormon, the CEO asked me to lie to a customer about our capabilities, which I refused to do. I had been prepared by revelation to know that the leaders of my company would "cause [me] to err." I began quietly looking in earnest for new opportunities and ended up changing coasts and moving to Maryland about six months later to take the job that I currently have at the National Institute of Standards and Technology.

Almost three months to the day that I left, a majority of the employees including the founder of the company were laid off by the new CEO – right before the Christmas holidays. I have kept in touch with some of my former co-workers – and for many of them their careers and their personal finances were significantly impacted by this layoff.

My family's emotional and physical welfare was protected in 1999 and many times since then because of reading, heeding, and applying revelation received from regular scripture study. I often ask myself - what would have happened if I had not been reading the Book of Mormon on a daily basis? How might my life and career be different today?

I express my gratitude to the prophet Nephi for recording the words of Isaiah in 2 Nephi 19:16 so that when I read them on that March morning more than two decades ago I would know what I needed to do. My family has been protected and blessed because of scripture study and application.

Start Reading!

I had the opportunity to speak at BYU Idaho in May 2014 when Elder Clark was then president of that wonderful school. The talk I gave for the University Forum, entitled "Facing Closed Doors" (see Chapter 12), discussed the effort that is sometimes required to succeed in our goals.

If you are someone who has drifted from the iron rod, I invite you to face that closed door – or that closed book! Knock on the door of heaven. Open your scriptures. Tap your Gospel Library app.

President Ezra Taft Benson taught: "Often we spend great effort in trying to increase the activity levels in our stakes. We work diligently to raise the percentages of those attending sacrament meetings. We labor to get a higher percentage of our young men on missions. We strive to improve the numbers of those marrying in the temple. All of these are commendable efforts and important to the growth of the kingdom. But <u>when individual members and families immerse themselves in the scriptures regularly and consistently, these other areas of activity will automatically come.</u> Testimonies will increase. Commitment will be strengthened. Families will be fortified. Personal revelation will flow (*Teachings of Ezra Taft Benson*, p. 44).

I know for myself, independent of any other person, that the Book of Mormon is true. And from this knowledge, I know that Jesus is the Christ and that Joseph Smith is His Prophet called to open the final dispensation. Because of my testimony of the Book of Mormon, I know that this is the Church of Jesus Christ and that we have a living prophet today who leads and guides this Church by revelation. I pray that each of us may make a commitment to regular personal and family scripture study so that we may experience the greater light and knowledge that our Heavenly Father wants to give to us.

Where much is given, much is required (D&C 82:3)! We carry in our smart phones and have on our bookshelves the greatest scriptural library in the history of the world. The Lord expects us to use these revelatory resources to survive the challenging times in which we live. Speaking of the Book of Mormon which he sees in vision, the prophet Nephi shares in 2 Nephi 28:2 that "the book shall be of great worth unto the children of men." I invite you to reflect on "what is the Book of Mormon worth to you?"

Chapter 11

Keeping on the Covenant Path with Vigilance and Precision

"they were perfectly honest and upright in all things"
– Alma 27:27

The 2,060 stripling warriors led by the prophet-general Helaman came from homes where their parents were perfectly honest and upright in all things. Being up and doing is something we learn in our homes. In your home, are you striving with vigilance and precision to keep on the covenant path?

Walt Disney World Has No Mosquitoes

Walt Disney World is the most visited vacation resort in the world with an average annual attendance prior to the current pandemic of almost 60 million people. When the resort was being built more than 50 years ago, the developers had a major problem to solve – mosquitoes! For you see, Walt Disney World is built on a 25,000 acre swamp in Orlando, Florida – and swamps typically come with lots of bugs and disease-carrying mosquitoes.

Walt Disney recognized that bites from mosquitoes would be annoying and even dangerous to visitors. If you have ever visited Disney World, you will find that there are essentially *no* mosquitoes. What would appear on the surface to be a miracle is rather a carefully engineered effort to maintain a pleasing environment for visitors. My family and I have been to Disney World three or four times. I do not recall ever once getting a mosquito bite. In fact, when we were there at this so-called "Happiest Place on Earth", we never even thought about the potential problem of mosquitoes. I learned that Disney's creative management of this problem takes place quietly behind the scenes. Likewise so much of what we do to stay on the covenant path is done behind the scenes through quiet, private acts that others do not see.

Efforts to Eliminate Mosquitoes at Walt Disney World

The methods used to accomplish this Disney "magic" are instructive and can also be correlated to our efforts to be truly converted to the Gospel of Jesus Christ and our personal progress on the covenant path. Likewise in our lives, little actions on our part can help us progress on the covenant path and the ongoing fight we have with sin in this fallen world.

To solve a problem like mosquitoes, you need the right expertise. Walt Disney hired an engineer and retired army general named Joe Potter[16] who had previously worked in the Panama Canal Zone and had successfully eliminated malaria-harboring mosquitoes there. Disney and Potter realized that the key was not to kill these pesky bugs once they got into the theme parks but to prevent the mosquitoes from getting there in the first place. Thus, from the beginning the designers' focus was on making Disney World an area that would be inhospitable for mosquitoes to lay their eggs rather than putting all of their energies into trying to kill adult mosquitoes.

The key for Disney World to eliminate mosquitoes – and for us to progress on the covenant path – is *living water*. Mosquitoes lay their eggs in standing, stagnant water. Likewise, if we become stagnant in our faith and devotion, the seeds of sins can drag us down or hatch into habits that pull us off the covenant path.

---

[16] https://insidethemagic.net/2019/08/no-mosquitoes-disney-world-bb1/ and https://www.mentalfloss.com/article/548281/reason-why-there-are-no-mosquitoes-in-disney-world

If we are to move forward along the covenant path, we must rely on *living water* from a living Savior. Remember what Jesus taught the Samaritan woman at the well in John 4:13-14 – "Jesus answered and said unto her, Whosoever drinketh of this water shall thirst again: But whosoever drinketh of the water that I shall give him shall never thirst; but the water that I shall give him shall be in him a well of water springing up into everlasting life."

Returning to Disney's challenge with mosquitoes – how did Disney World obtain living water to eliminate mosquito incubators?

- First, they dug drainage canals to remove any stagnant water and reclaim the swamp land
- In Florida where Disney World is located, it often rains – typically over 50 inches each year – so additional ditches were built throughout the park grounds to remove any water before it can pool and become stagnant
- Buildings in the Disney theme parks were carefully designed with curves and other features to prevent areas where any draining water might pool and become stagnant
- Any intentional water inside the parks is <u>always on the move</u>, which is why you see so many fountains with flowing water around the Magic Kingdom and the other theme parks
- In addition, plants throughout the park are carefully placed and do not have leaves that would harbor stagnant water after it rains

Sin is like the mosquitoes – seeking to bite, annoy, or destroy us if we do not eliminate opportunities for it to flourish in our lives. This is why we must be up and doing to keep on the covenant path.

What if some mosquitoes do make it into Disney?

- Natural predators of mosquitos are maintained on the site
- For example, any bodies of water around the Disney World properties are regularly stocked with goldfish, minnows, and other fish that eat mosquito larvae
- Apparently rather than using traditional pesticides, a liquid garlic spray, which is harmless to humans, is used to deter mosquitoes. This spray is regularly spread around the parks particularly at sunrise and sunset when mosquitoes would be most active
- The Disney Mosquito Surveillance Program includes traps to capture and study any bugs that make it past the other security measures – and these data are used to make adjustments to spraying patterns and other mosquito killing methods
- In addition, across the Disney properties, "sentinel chickens" are kept behind the scenes in coops where their blood is actively monitored for mosquito-borne diseases. By keeping a careful and constant watch, any significant mosquito infestation can be prevented.

As one source[17] I found stated: "[Disney doesn't] have any particularly special weapon that isn't used elsewhere in the world... On their own, they're all methods that many other places employ to deal with the annoying bugs. However the impressive part is the vigilance and precision in which Disney carries out these methods."

Vigilance and Precision Needed to Stay on the Covenant Path

We require vigilance and precision in our efforts to get on and stay on the covenant path back to our heavenly home, which is an activity far more important to our eternal salvation and exaltation than eliminating pesky mosquitoes at the world's busiest amusement park.

---

[17] See https://www.youtube.com/watch?v=_30jPKzWdN0&feature=youtu.be

In the world, mosquitoes are always there waiting for an opportunity to breed and bite and annoy. Similarly the forces trying to draw us off the covenant path are always there waiting for an opportunity to injure our spirits – to breed, to bite, and to annoy.

I invite you to regularly review the temple recommend questions. Your responses to them will help you stay on the covenant path. President Nelson shared these questions in his October 2019 General Conference closing remarks[18] – and thus they are available to each of us.

In this same talk, President Nelson shared: "In addition to their answering those questions honestly, it is understood that each adult temple patron will wear the sacred garment of the priesthood under their regular clothing. This is symbolic of an inner commitment to strive each day to become more like the Lord. It also reminds us to remain faithful each day to covenants made and to walk on the covenant path each day in a higher and holier way."

President Nelson continued: "Individual worthiness to enter the Lord's house requires much individual spiritual preparation. But with the Lord's help, nothing is impossible. In some respects, it is easier to build a temple than it is to build a people prepared for a temple. Individual worthiness requires a total conversion of mind and heart to be more like the Lord, to be an honest citizen, to be a better example, and to be a holier person."

May each of us give heed to the invitation of a living prophet and be up and doing – acting with vigilance and precision – in keeping on the covenant path.

---

[18] https://www.churchofjesuschrist.org/study/general-conference/2019/10/57nelson?lang=eng

Chapter 12

Facing Closed Doors:
Pressing Forward After Failures

"by his grace…we have power to do these things [perform miracles]"
– Jacob 4:7

When you are up and doing, you sometimes fail. How you respond when you face these failures, what may seem to be "closed doors" at the time, will make all the difference in your life! Continue to press forward, to seek, and to knock. This message was given as a BYU Idaho University Forum on May 15, 2014 (see https://web.byui.edu/DevotionalsAndSpeeches/).

I am deeply honored and grateful for the opportunity to speak to you today. As students at BYU Idaho you are fortunate to be regularly taught by amazing people who have led interesting lives. While I will not make the claim to be amazing, I pray that my message today can touch your heart and inspire you in your studies and in your life.

I can still recall what I learned and felt at my first university forum while a student at Brigham Young University in the fall of 1987. The speaker was Elder L. Tom Perry of the Quorum of the Twelve Apostles. The date was September 17, 1987 – the 200th anniversary of the signing of the United States Constitution. Since I have always loved U.S. history, I came to the forum early and sat up front. I stayed after the talk was done and went forward to meet Elder Perry. This was my first opportunity to shake an Apostle's hand at BYU. I thanked him for his message. However, it was the event after the forum that forever changed me.

As I was one of the last people to leave the Marriott Center that day, I unexpectedly found myself walking next to BYU President

Jeffrey R. Holland who was returning to his office. We walked together for about two blocks and had several minutes to converse which consisted of President Holland primarily asking me questions – my name, how I was enjoying school, and so forth. As a freshman who had been at BYU for less than a month, I was amazed that the president of the university would actually talk to me and care enough to ask me questions about myself. I felt loved and appreciated. I have only met Elder Holland one other time.

In November 2001, he came to our stake in Maryland to teach me and other stake leaders the roles and responsibilities of a bishop, a calling that I received less than six months later. Because of our earlier encounter, I felt a special connection to Elder Holland as if he had come to our stake to specifically train and prepare me. You never know the impact you can have on the life of another person. Maybe even something you will hear today will make a difference in your life. I hope so.

I graduated from college more than 20 years ago. My, has the world changed over the past two decades! This afternoon I thought I might offer a David Letterman style Top Ten list of things that differ today from when I graduated from BYU in 1992.

Top Ten...Things that differ today from when I graduated from BYU in 1992

Number 10. Google was a number not a verb – it was simply a 1 followed by 100 zeros.

Number 9. Tweeting was something that birds did – and they weren't angry birds!

Number 8. Cell phones were the size of your shoe – and were only used for making phone calls – very expensive phone calls.

Number 7. Homework assignments were turned in on paper and we looked up information in books found in libraries.

Number 6. Computers had floppy disks about the size of a slice of bread and were not networked.

Number 5. O.J. Simpson was only famous as a football player.

Number 4. Cameras had film and no one knew what a "selfie" was.

Number 3. Texting wasn't even a word – much less a primary means of communication.

Number 2. Without GPS navigation, women stopped at gas stations to ask for directions and men got lost!

And the number one thing that differs today from 20 years ago: The internet – the internet was still a figment of Al Gore's imagination.

In discussing some of the points I wish to make today, I hope you will allow me to share some things about myself. This will give you an opportunity to get to know me a little better, which may be helpful later when we open the floor to questions. Perhaps some of my life's lessons can help you with yours.

Facing Closed Doors

I have entitled my remarks today "Facing Closed Doors." Those who have been on full-time missions know something about this topic. I faced many closed doors, closed minds, and closed hearts in Boston, Massachusetts[i] where I served from 1988 to 1990. I knew well the anxiety of anticipation as I approached those doors in Massachusetts. Would anyone be home? Would they greet me or reject me? Or would they just ignore me, pretending they didn't hear our knock?

There will come times in your life when you come to doors that you want to enter that are closed. How you react may determine whether or not you are able to go through that door. The question I want to explore today is - when faced with a closed door, what do you do? Do you give up or do you persistently knock? Do you have faith that the door will open when appropriate for it to do so?

In the popular Disney movie *Frozen*, little princess Anna knocks on her older sister Elsa's closed door time and time again while they are growing up. Anna knocks each time with enthusiasm and faith that the door will open! You have to admire her persistence and sustained energy over the many attempts that she makes to get her sister's attention as she simply asks, "Do *you* want to build a snowman?"

True, there are more important things to build in life than snowmen – and often more challenging doors to open. However, the approach we take with doors that are temporarily closed needs to include persistence, faith, and sustained energy and enthusiasm if we wish to discover the treasures and opportunities that lie behind them as we journey through life.

In the winter months of early 1992 as I was nearing completion on my undergraduate chemistry degree at BYU, I like many of you was faced with the decision of what to do with my life and my schooling. Most concerning was that I was approaching my BYU graduation as an unmarried man! *That* was more terrifying than facing the GRE, graduate school applications or my final exams!

You see the first devotional talk I had attended at BYU had been delivered by Elder M. Russell Ballard who had shared that unmarried men were a "menace to society" and had quoted Lehi in 2 Nephi 1:21 "arise from the dust, my sons, and be men…" Elder Ballard's talk had not bothered me at the time because I was getting ready to go on a mission. But now, five years later, as a graduating senior, I was about to leave "Happy Valley" in Provo for the unknown – and possibly the scant dating opportunities of some far away graduate school with few Mormon girls.

I had grown up in a little town in Missouri where there were almost no other LDS kids my age – so I knew that similar to the probability of a chemical reaction occurring where you need a sufficient number of molecules to create a reaction, you need to have sufficient number of dating possibilities if you are going to get married. I needed to go to a place where there were potential LDS women that I could marry – and where I could pursue a career that interested me. I needed to go to the right place.

When I was deciding more than 20 years ago on which graduate school to attend to pursue a career in forensic science, we did not have the internet available to us. Today you can obtain answers to questions you have in seconds with a Google search on your smart phone. But Larry Page and Sergey Brin, the founders of Google, were not even graduate students themselves and had not yet thought of the Google search engine much less developed it into the powerful tool that it is today. And smart phones were still an Apple in Steve Jobs' eye and would not be developed for another 15 years! Yes, I am very old – and from some student's perspectives probably lived before the dawn of time – or at least before the dawn of texting!

My graduate school search involved going to the BYU Library and reviewing a big red book that contained all of the graduate chemistry programs and professors in the United States and the principal papers they had published. With a prayer in my heart, I reviewed EVERY page – every line - of this more than 500 page book with very small print. I can still recall scanning those pages for hours evening after evening searching for the right place to apply. I was interested in forensic science; a topic that has only become popular in recent years due to now abundant TV shows such as *CSI: Crime Scene Investigation, Forensic Files,* or *Bones.* I knew what I wanted, but I did not know where to go. What graduate school door would open when I knocked?

During my search I found the name of a professor at the University of Virginia near the back of the book who had published some work in forensic science. Sometimes I wonder how my life would be different if I had not persisted through that struggle but instead had stopped searching at the University of Alabama or the University of Arizona near the front of the book. The detailed search I performed provided valuable perspective regarding the entirety of graduate chemistry programs in the United States. I knew what I wanted better because of all that I had been through in my search.

I decided to apply to the University of Virginia because of my discovery of this professor named Ralph Allen who had published some interesting work in forensic science and had won several awards from the FBI for his work. One of my goals at the time was to work in the FBI Laboratory, since it was the best place in the country to do forensic science research.

The story behind my initial visit to the University of Virginia is instructive. Graduate schools typically invite potential students to visit their campus on a specific weekend where the accepted students can get to know one another as well as the professors. Graduate school is a different environment in many ways from an undergraduate education. Graduate students often provide an important part of the workforce for a university and strong bonds can form between professors and their students because of time spent together. My father, who himself was a university professor at the time, emphasized that choosing *the right professor* is even more important than choosing the right school.

At the University of Virginia, graduate students are often lured by serving them lots of alcohol particularly on the invited weekend. I found out later that the school can spend thousands of dollars getting potential students drunk in trying to get them to have a good time. UVA has in the past received the dubious honor of being the number one party school in the country. You can imagine that going from BYU which is regularly ranked the number one "stone cold sober" school to the University of Virginia with its abundant alcohol and other vices was a shock to my system. But after watching fellow students get plastered and deal with hangovers at UVA, my commitment to live the Word of Wisdom only grew stronger!

At the time I was looking at graduate schools, I was preparing to run the Boston Marathon. On the weekend set aside for prospective graduate students to visit the campus, I was planning on running the Canyonlands Half Marathon in Moab, Utah in preparation for the Boston Marathon the following month. I contacted the University of Virginia and told them that I needed to come a different week than the time when all of the other accepted students would be there. This unknowingly turned out to be a great blessing in many ways. Not only did I miss the crowds and entertaining, I was also able to gain a more realistic perspective of the University's environment.

Because I was interested in working with a specific professor, I asked to meet with Professor Ralph Allen during my visit to Virginia. However, I was told that Dr. Allen was now in administration and was no longer accepting any graduate students – and in fact had not had any graduate students for more than four years. This was very discouraging! I had searched the entire country via the graduate chemistry program book. I had prayed and sought the Lord's guidance on what I should do. I had located the one person I wanted to study under only to be told that he is not taking any students. With faith and persistence, I continued to enthusiastically knock on this "closed" door. Perhaps I could have sung, "Do you want to build a graduate student?"

My reply to the University of Virginia was simply, "I am not coming to visit your school unless you give me an opportunity to speak with Dr. Allen." This was rather bold considering that I was one of several dozen accepted graduate students. They did not need me. I really had no leverage – and I had blown off the school already in terms of refusing to come when the other accepted graduate students were visiting. Finally, I received word that Dr. Allen was willing to meet with me if I would come visit the University of Virginia the weekend after all of the other students were coming.

So the last weekend in March 1992, I flew from Utah to Virginia and drove to Charlottesville. Flowers and trees were blooming. Bees were buzzing, sweet birds singing, there was music ringing in the air… ☺ I discovered that truly there is no place on earth more beautiful than central Virginia in spring. I fell in love with this area.

When I arrived at the University, Dr. Allen took me to Quantico, to the FBI Academy, where he was in charge of the accreditation of forensic science courses being taught there – something I did not know when I originally contacted him. He also told me he could get me into the FBI Laboratory as a visiting scientist where I would be able to do my graduate research.

That sealed it. I decided to attend the University of Virginia – and that has made all the difference in my life. I finished my courses at BYU in August of 1992, then started in Charlottesville the next month and in May 1993 began working at Quantico, where I stayed for the next two years. I lived at Quantico and worked in their forensic science research unit – first as an FBI Honors Intern and then as a visiting scientist. This door opened to me at precisely the same time that the wave was just breaking on forensic DNA analysis, and I was able to surf that wave and apply my interest in instrumentation and developing new technologies.

A year after I arrived in Virginia another door opened and I met my future wife. I will discuss this topic further a little later.

Be Willing to Pay the Price

In my field of forensic DNA analysis, the advances have been amazing to observe and to participate in over the past 20 years. TV programs such as *CSI* and *Law & Order* make forensic science appear rapid, easy and always successful in solving crimes. Unfortunately, reality is far from Hollywood's projection of instant and absolute results. *Forensic science requires, as all science does, time and hard work – but the thrill of discovery brings great satisfaction.*

A lot has changed since the early days of forensic DNA analysis. DNA tests used at the time of the O.J. Simpson trial almost 20 years ago took about 8 weeks to perform and required significant amounts of blood or other body fluids for identification. Forensic DNA testing today can be performed in less than 8 hours – and soon hopefully in less than an hour. These DNA tests require only a few cells such as may be left in a single fingerprint.

I have been able to play a role in these technological advancements and now help to train up the next generation of scientists. Behind that door that opened for me at the FBI, I found more opportunities to learn, discover, and share as other doors led me to new destinations. What will you do with the education you have received? What door will you knock on next? Which one will you step through? What impact will your efforts have in making the world a better place?

What happens if the door you thought you were supposed to go through does not open? Or if the path on the other side takes an unexpected turn or becomes too rocky to navigate? How do you develop that faith to go forward following a failure? When something goes wrong, do not give up. Work in science is called research or – re-search – because it is a quest that often needs to be repeated. Your experiments, an article you write, or the computer code you create may not work the first time. You cannot let failure defeat you. Rather let it propel you forward with renewed innovation and commitment to succeed. Seek out and embrace your own scientific problems to solve and illuminate your part of the world with your unique collection of knowledge, talents, and determination.

I have always appreciated a quote from President Calvin Coolidge: "Nothing in the world can take the place of persistence. Talent will not; nothing is more common than unsuccessful men with talent. Genius will not; unrewarded genius is almost a proverb. … Persistence and determination alone are omnipotent. The slogan 'Press on' has solved and always will solve the problems of the human race."[ii]

While in college I got the crazy idea that I wanted to qualify for and run in the Boston Marathon. Although I had run cross country and track in high school, preparing for a 26.2 mile race was a little daunting since I had never run more than about five or six miles at a time. I developed a 3- month training plan and began running six days a week. In my first marathon, I hit the "wall" at mile 24 and ended up walking the last two miles. I finished 12 minutes short of the required qualifying time for Boston.

Now I could have considered myself a failure and given up on my goal to run in the most prestigious marathon in the world. Many people would probably be happy to just finish a marathon at all, which I had done. Instead, I was determined to try again and do whatever I had to do to reach my goal. I began more intense training. Running close to 2,000 miles over the next year, I devoted sometimes two hours a day to improve my stamina and speed. When I ran my next marathon, I finished more than 31 minutes faster – easily surpassing the qualifying time for Boston. The following April, [April 20, 1992] I ran in the 96th Boston Marathon. Achieving this goal was a significant milestone in my life – and I often reflect on what I learned from this experience.

This persistence in spite of initial failure has benefited my scientific work as well. During my graduate research, at the FBI Academy, I learned how to perform the polymerase chain reaction, or PCR. This is a widely-used process in molecular biology to replicate or create copies of specific DNA sequences, much like the way rumors are spread: you tell two friends and they tell two friends and so on.

In my early experimental work, I could not get the PCR reaction to work properly for several weeks. I performed dozens of experiments day after day changing the various components of the DNA test. I persisted in my experiments and eventually succeeded in finding and fixing the problem. These initial failures required me to break down and examine every part of the PCR process. This effort led to a detailed understanding of the process – something that has benefited me throughout my career and laid the groundwork for my expertise in DNA analysis. If everything had worked the first time, I would have missed a valuable learning experience – the fruits of which I now share with scientists all over the world to help them in their work, too.

The former head of NASA, Daniel Goldin, has said: "Not experiencing any failure in life is rarely a sign of perfection; rather it is a sign that your goals aren't bold enough... The real mark of your character comes from not how you react to your successes, ...[but] how you react to your failures."[iii]

There is Value in Trials and Tribulation

Joseph Smith regularly taught that God will have a tried people[iv]. D&C Sections 121, 122, and 123 teach about perspective that comes from tribulation. All of us will fail at something we attempt to do in our life. *It is how you respond to that failure that will determine the measure of the man or woman you become.* It is in failure that we learn and gain experience. You may fail to fulfill an assignment as quickly or completely as is needed by others. You may fail to reach a goal you have set. The only way you will not experience failure is to do nothing – and then you ARE a failure! My wife recalled a quote she saw hanging on the wall of her physics classroom when she was in high school that read: "We must learn not to let our fear of failure make us fail and we must not allow our fears to make our failures final." Continue to knock on doors that may appear closed with faith, enthusiasm, and hard work.

Thomas Edison, the most successful inventor in U.S. history, explored thousands of ways to make a light bulb, enduring failure after failure before he succeeded in illuminating the world. Edison is credited with the famous saying: "Genius is one percent inspiration, ninety-nine percent perspiration."[v] That perspiration comes from hard work and sometimes failing more than succeeding. Attitude makes a difference here. Regarding his many experiments that did not work, Edison noted: "I have not failed. I've just found 10,000 ways that won't work."[vi] It is likely that your next door will not open until you have conquered the problem or learned the lesson in the room you are in now.

Another valuable experience I have learned about stepping through open doors is to pause, turn around and thank the one who turned the knob and opened the door before looking to the next room. Always credit your sources because you truly stand on the shoulders of others to accomplish anything in life. I chose a scientific career in large measure because of a diligent and dedicated high school biology teacher named Kermit Posten. Mr. Posten demanded excellence of his students. His lectures were fact-filled. His tests were challenging. He expected us to do our best. Perhaps you have had a teacher like this that has challenged and inspired you. Mr. Posten instilled in me a desire to learn and to love biology. I began as his student at a small high school in Maryville, Missouri. Now I am the teacher and the world is my classroom.

Seven years ago I tracked down Mr. Posten. He still lives in that small Missouri town. I thanked him for inspiring my scientific career with a signed copy of my latest textbook. I will always cherish that moment when I had the opportunity to thank my teacher and mentor – one who believed in me and set me on a path of success.

I am here today because I did not give up when I initially failed with some projects. But also I am here because others have not given up on me. Remember that nothing you do in life will be accomplished solely through your efforts. You are always building on the knowledge and experience of others. Be grateful for them. Be grateful that you are not alone, and tell them so.

Always Keep Learning

The doors that lead you through your education should not stop with receipt of a diploma. Your true education BEGINS with college graduation. College teaches you how to learn. Life after college enables you to develop your learning skills and to apply them to real problems.

I love to learn. The desire to learn from everything around me is a passion that I have had all my life. I became a scientist because I like solving puzzles. Scientific research involves solving some amazing puzzles. I enjoy the thrill of discovery. I cherish those moments when understanding comes as pieces of a challenging problem solidify into a satisfying solution.

Regardless of how much you put into study, there will still be many thousands of hours of learning required over a lifetime to achieve your best in your field of endeavor. I cannot emphasize enough the importance of self-education. I have never had a single class on molecular biology or statistics – yet I have written books that included both subjects. How? I have read extensively and taught myself. I concur with Thomas Jefferson who wrote to John Adams late in his life: "I cannot live without books."[vii]

We are each unique – blessed with talents and experiences that can make a difference to those around you. Unless you have an identical twin, your DNA – your genetic blueprint – is unique. There is literally no one else in the world quite like you. Seek to know how your specific characteristics and gifts are meant to make this world a better place.

Courageously face your future failures with resilience, resolve, and determination. Show appreciation and share your successes with those who have helped you. And always, always keep learning! If you keep learning, no failure is final. And no doors remain closed.

Fear of Speaking

Sometimes our fears are so great that they prevent us from even approaching the door step. Many people have a fear of public speaking. According to a 2013 study[viii] from the National Institute of Mental Health, 74 % of people surveyed suffer from speech anxiety. I used to be one of them. I was terrified of standing in front of other people. In fact, during my first school speech in seventh grade English class, I broke down crying during my talk. I resolved after that experience that I would face that fear – and overcome it.

It was not easy. In high school, I had a public speaking class teacher who was willing to work with me. She spent hours with me after school. I think Mrs. Kinman has a place reserved in heaven for putting up with me! I entered every speech contest available in high school and while I did not win any first place prizes, I kept trying – and improving. I also took a public speaking class at BYU even though it was not required. I knew I would need to go through that door if I wanted to reach my goals in life.

I am grateful for the help of patient teachers, enduring fellow students and kind and attentive audience members. I am above all thankful for my loving Father in Heaven who has answered my many prayers for strength offered each time before I speak. Develop your talents even if this means facing your fears! Not only will your confidence grow, but your fears will diminish and you will discover more potential than you ever thought you could have.

My first scientific talk was given a little over 20 years ago in a hotel ballroom in Frederick, Maryland. After months of collecting data, I stayed up all night long finishing my slides and trying to get everything ready for this important presentation. The big day finally arrived. I was excited. I was nervous. I was terrified. I did not want to break down crying during my talk. To add to my nervousness, the person introducing me thought I was a "professor" from the University of Virginia rather than a graduate student -- and I had to correct this when I began my talk.

During the middle of my presentation while I was showing the chemical structure of a new compound used for improving detection of DNA, someone in the audience of several hundred people yelled out: "Hey, that carbon has five bonds to it. That can't be right!" As I turned to look at the slide more closely, I realized this critic was correct. In my sleep-deprived state of the all-nighter when I was completing my slides, I had drawn the chemical structure incorrectly!

It is impossible to convey the horror that I felt in that moment. I felt as though the door to my future career in science was not just being closed – it was being slammed shut! Now I wanted to break down crying! Fortunately, I think with a little help from heaven, I tried to lighten the mood of this tense moment by replying: "Yes, you are correct. That carbon does have five bonds. I must have developed some new chemistry!" And then with the audience laughing I opened that "closed" door and finished my talk.

I left that experience a different person. I committed to myself that this type of mistake would *never* happen again. I committed to meticulously pay attention to every detail in slide presentations I give. I have made tens of thousands of PowerPoint slides since then – and I am happy to report that all my carbons now have four bonds!

The prophet Moroni reminds us in Ether 12:27 that coming unto our Savior Jesus Christ is key to entering a closed door. "And if men come unto me I will show unto them their weakness. I give unto men weakness that they may be humble; and my grace is sufficient for all men that humble themselves before me; for it they humble themselves before me, and have faith in me, then will I make weak things become strong unto them." The prophet Jacob recorded in Jacob 4:7: "Nevertheless, the Lord God showeth us our weakness that we may know that it is by his grace, and his great condescensions unto the children of men, that we have power to do these things."

Since that first scientific presentation in October 1993, I have had the opportunity to give more than 300 presentations on five continents and in 22 countries so far. I am grateful that with the help of good teachers, many hours of hard work and preparation, and blessings from above, I have faced and opened the closed door that was my fear of public speaking. Otherwise it would not be possible for me to be speaking to you today. You, too, can face fears and these closed doors can open as you knock and make a concerted effort to enter.

As my confidence in speaking was beginning to rise, so also did the bar of my aspirations. Daydreams of what I wished I could do someday grew into goals I believed I could really achieve.

Speaking at the Book of Mormon Symposium

As a student at BYU, I loved attending the many symposiums and conferences held at the school. One of these was the Book of Mormon Symposium. Over the course of nine years from 1986 to 1994 gospel scholars and Church Educational System instructors shared their insights regarding the Book of Mormon section by section.

During my attendance at one of these talks after my mission, I somehow got the cockamamie idea that I should prepare and give a presentation at this BYU Book of Mormon Symposium. I shared this desire with a roommate and other close friends. I think they were a bit skeptical. I was just a peon chemistry student. What insights might I have to share when distinguished religion professors were the ones who always gave these presentations? Robert Matthews, Robert Millet, Joseph Fielding McConkie and others were the regular invited speakers.

Undeterred, I faced this closed door and eyed it with curious wonder. As I started graduate school in Virginia, the idea of participating in the BYU Book of Mormon Symposium would not leave me. I decided to knock. After many, many hours of research and writing, I prepared a manuscript and submitted my idea. The rejection letter reached me about a month later. I was disappointed and discouraged. Getting a rejection letter is never fun. Why couldn't this door open for me? Didn't I deserve a chance to share something I knew about the Book of Mormon?

I decided to persist and to knock again the next year. I began to develop my idea about six months before the fall submission deadline. Again hours and hours of research and writing were conducted. I learned so much during the process of my intense study. I began to realize that even if I did not get an opportunity to speak at the BYU Symposium, I was benefiting from my study and preparation. The goal and the dream of speaking on the Book of Mormon drove me forward in my studies. I found that my love and admiration for the Book of Mormon grew as I studied it intently. I completed and was satisfied with my proposed manuscript. I wondered as I sent my paper off for evaluation and consideration if this door would open for me.

Much to my surprise and delight, an acceptance letter arrived a few weeks later! In February 1994, I returned to BYU for the first time since I had graduated to deliver a presentation comparing the prophet Mormon to the prophet Joseph Smith in a talk entitled "The 'Author' and the 'Finisher' of the Book of Mormon." Of 40 presenters at the ninth and final Book of Mormon Symposium, only 25 were selected for publication. My article appears as chapter 5 in that book[ix]. The author byline reads "John M. Butler is a (peon) graduate student at the University of Virginia…" ☺ Dream. Work. Knock. The right doors will open for you with persistence and faith and hard work. The fruits of studying the Book of Mormon paid off in a dream come true. Little did I know then that about ten years more of continued scripture study would lead me to the door of an adjoining room that would test me in a different way – and use my preparation to help others.

The Q → K Comparison

I think about and use comparisons a lot in my life. Forensic science is based on comparisons of a sample in question or a "question" sample (Q) with a known sample (K). We call this the Q-to-K comparison. An evidence sample is compared back to a known reference sample to see if any associations can be made. In the case of forensic DNA testing, the Q sample comes from the evidence at a crime scene while the K sample is collected from a suspect or perhaps multiple suspects in some circumstances.

The important point here is that without the reference or known sample, no comparison can be made. Like the game of Memory involving many pairs of matching cards, if we have results from a crime scene but there is no suspect to which to compare our results, then we simply cannot make the match and solve the crime. Unfortunately, many crimes are never solved because there is no known reference sample to which the evidence result can be compared.

Likewise, the Q-to-K comparison is performed in paternity testing when an alleged father's DNA profile is compared to a child's DNA profile to see if he can possibly be the child's father – and thus be required to pay child support.

Disaster victims are identified using a similar approach. For example, if a plane crashes, then bodies of victims can be identified through comparing DNA results from the victim's recovered remains to DNA results from parents or other relatives. Without DNA from relatives or a direct reference sample from a toothbrush or comb the victim may have left at home, they cannot be identified. There must be a reference sample for comparison purposes.

With this Q-to-K comparison in mind, let us connect the topics of DNA and the Book of Mormon.

DNA and the Book of Mormon

Starting around the year 2001 some vocal critics of the Church began touting that DNA studies of Native American people could prove the Book of Mormon false. Their argument was that DNA research studies have shown that almost all Native Americans alive today have DNA that can be associated most closely with DNA from Asian people. This scientific research supports the migration model that the Americas were initially populated via the Bering Strait between Siberia and Alaska when this region was a land bridge more than 15,000 years ago. Thus, in the Church critics' minds without a direct DNA match in Native Americans today back to Jewish, Middle Eastern DNA, there is no scientific support for the journey of Lehi's family from Jerusalem to the New World.

At first glance, science and the gospel may appear to be incompatible. Should we then close the doors on our testimony of the Book of Mormon because of some scientific studies – in this case DNA results of Native Americans? Certainly critics of the Church make it seem that way.

As a DNA scientist, how can I face what appears to be a closed door to Book of Mormon authenticity? Well, I faced this "closed" door the same way I have faced all of the other closed doors in my life – by knocking and intense studying. I began asking questions of the Book of Mormon and seeking to understand what the record itself says about the genetic ancestry of its people. Years of study and research on both DNA and the Book of Mormon put me in a unique position to step through another open door, to set the record straight, and to clear the cobwebs of confusion that had begun to form in the minds of the curious.

I learned that there had to be many other people in this Promised Land than just Lehi's family in order to meet the numbers specified in Nephi's early record. Who were they? What did their DNA look like? American history tells us that over the 1600 years since the close of the Book of Mormon record, epidemics of disease such as smallpox claimed the lives of entire populations. This loss of life complicates the ability to fully inform our genetic view of the past when testing modern Native American population groups. Most importantly, since we do not know anything about Lehi's DNA and genetic heritage, we cannot match it to populations of today. And where there is no known or "K" sample, we cannot answer the desired question. In other words, we cannot prove or disprove the Book of Mormon record with DNA studies from modern Native Americans.

Here is what I wrote on this matter in an article entitled "A Few Thoughts from a Believing DNA Scientist" published in November 2003 in the *Journal of Book of Mormon Studies*[x]: "While it is possible to speculate endlessly about scenarios that would make Book of Mormon story lines compatible with current DNA evidence, the record itself is simply not descriptive enough to provide definitive calibration points with which to make confident scientific conclusions. Thus, we are left where we started (and where I believe the Lord intended us to be) – in the realm of faith. A spiritual witness is the only way to know the truthfulness of the Book of Mormon. Although DNA studies have made links between Native Americans and Asians, these studies in no way invalidate the Book of Mormon despite the loud voices of detractors."

Answering Doctrinal Questions

To understand any truth we need anchors to start from. The standard works should serve as our reference calibration points in our gospel study. Doctrinal questions, like any scientific measurement, are best addressed by comparison to a known quantity. This is why the Book of Mormon, the Bible, the Doctrine and Covenants, and the Pearl of Great Price are so important. They serve as our reference calibration points for doctrinal questions we may have.

The Standard Works are called "standard" for a reason. They are the reference material by which we can know the Truth, the Way, and the Life. They are the rod of iron that guides us back to the Tree of Life. Once we have found our North Star, we can confidently chart our course onward, humbly learning along the way in preparation for what lies beyond the next door in our lives. If we do not invest the time and effort to learn, we will likely find ourselves regrettably unprepared to enter the next room.

Be Humble and Teachable

My father, Doug Butler, has been an educator all of his life. With my mother, who also has a college degree in teaching, he, through example and effort, raised and taught seven children of which I am the oldest. All seven of us are graduates of BYU or BYU Idaho. In his professional career, he has been a teacher for almost 45 years including teaching at three different universities while I was growing up. He and two of my brothers now run their own school in Northwestern Nebraska teaching students from all over the world how to work with horses' feet to keep them healthy and sure. Over the course of his career, my father has interacted with literally thousands of students, many of whom have traveled great distances to learn from him because he is widely regarded to be one of the world's best in his field.

When asked what qualities make students successful and teachable, my father commented: First, to be a good student and to be teachable, you must admit that you do not know anything. Now for some, the fact that we don't know anything may be quite evident to everyone else but ourselves! Pride prevents us from wanting to feel ignorant. The second principle of being teachable is that we must realize that learning is hard work. Just being exposed to new information does not mean that we learn anything.

Be a Front-Row Learner

Having had an opportunity to teach many classes in my lifetime, I have noticed that the closer someone sits to the teacher in a classroom, the more eager they are to learn. Thus to a large extent you can judge a person's desire to learn by how close they sit to the front of the classroom; a truly teachable person will come early, sit close, and stay awake and focused during a lesson or meeting.

Sitting close to the teacher not only helps one to hear better but also helps avoid noticing distractions that can occur in any teaching environment. When a student closes the gap physically to the teacher, they show desire to learn.

I first observed my wife Terilynne in a Church history class that we both took at BYU. She sat in the front row on the edge of her seat; she recorded the lectures; and she attended outside lectures to further her learning. When we had the class together I did not know her name, but I never forgot her attitude towards learning. We met serendipitously about two years later in Charlottesville, Virginia while I was attending graduate school. I just happened to end up in her home ward. It was after we began dating that I realized she was the same front-row enthusiastic learner that I remembered from my undergraduate Church history class. I asked her to marry me in large measure because I knew that she was teachable and had a great desire to learn. Anyone who knows her knows that she loves to listen and cares deeply about other people. She is a wonderful example to me of being a front-row learner!

A few weeks ago we celebrated 20 years of marriage. I am grateful for all that I have learned from her. Truly "love is an open door" as we are reminded in a song sung in the Disney film *Frozen*. The love of learning that we share has become a part of everything we do and has been a great blessing to our family and those we serve.

Learn. Act. Share. Become.

When I was called to be Young Men's president in our ward, I determined that I would be much more effective in engaging the young men in the Duty to God program if I accepted the challenge to complete it myself. This program has a three-part focus: learn, act, and share. These three topics also apply in science and in life as well as the gospel.

I especially enjoy the "share" portion. When you get to a certain point in your career, you may become the expert that people will turn to for help with questions. Unfortunately, some people in this situation due to pride decide not to help others but to use their knowledge to feather their own nest rather than building up and teaching others. However, my father taught me a truth that I have come to appreciate as I have taught others: "You don't truly learn anything until you have to teach it to someone else."[xi]

Sharing is service and brings great joy and satisfaction. I answer hundreds of emails each year from people all over the world asking questions about DNA. In taking the time to answer them, I am learning how to better answer questions. Concepts become clearer to me as I describe them to others. Thus, sharing leads to further learning – and opens doors to new knowledge.

As we learn, act, and share, we become better. This is the goal of why we are here on this earth. I find it interesting that Elder Bednar's three books follow this same Learn – Act – Share pattern: (1) *Increase in Learning*, (2) *Act in Doctrine*, and (3) *Power to Become*.

When we learn and improve, we qualify ourselves for the next opportunity to stretch and become more. We are prepared to meet the next door with faith and confidence that if we do so humbly, always relying on the Lord for guidance and strength, He will lead us across the threshold and into our next lab of learning. It may not be easy but then a walk in a park does not prepare us to climb mountains to one day take in a view of the universe.

Courage comes to those who raise their knuckles to knock. As the famous author and speaker Dale Carnegie has said: "Inaction breeds doubt and fear. Action breeds confidence and courage. If you want to conquer fear, do not sit home and think about it. Go out and get busy!"[xii]

Final Thoughts

Are we committed to move forward and to face doors that seem closed at the time? We are here today because of the courage and faith of a young boy who in the spring of 1820 was willing to face closed doors. Ask – seek – knock. Learn. Act. Share.

In a grove of trees now called sacred, young Joseph Smith knelt and knocked on the door of heaven. In the initial moments of his attempts to pray, thick darkness gathered around. To young Joseph in those initial frightful moments as he sought wisdom from God the door to heaven probably seemed closed. But he persisted – and so must we. It will make all the difference in our lives.

Young Joseph's knock was answered in the Sacred Grove. His First Vision opened the heavens and the latter-day work that we are a part of today. I am also grateful that Joseph Smith was willing to face with faith doors of friendship that closed after he shared his experience.

I am grateful for the doors I have had to face over the years as I have learned so much from facing them and knocking and entering when the time was right. Perhaps behind what seem to you today to be closed doors await graduate school, a fulfilling career, a mission, marriage, or even a future opportunity to speak to students at a great university!

May you face your closed doors like Princess Anna did in *Frozen* – with faith, enthusiasm, and perseverance. And may they open when the time is right for them to do so. I know that what the Savior taught is true when He said: "Therefore, ask, and ye shall receive; knock, and it shall be opened unto you unto you; for he that asketh, receiveth; and unto him that knocketh, it shall be opened"[xiii]. And so will it be for you.

---

i Unfortunately, I never met President Clark when I was there in Boston but Clayton Christensen was the bishop of one of the wards I served in and was a strong supporter of missionary work!

ii http://en.wikiquote.org/wiki/Calvin_Coolidge; Calvin Coolidge was the 30th President of the United States and lived from 1872 to 1933.

iii Daniel S. Goldin in his commencement speech —Galileo and the Search for Truth to Massachusetts Institute of Technology graduates in 2001. Complete speech is available at http://www.humanity.org/voices/commencements/daniel-goldin-mit-speech-2001.

iv See *Teachings of the Prophet Joseph Smith*, p. 134-135

v http://en.wikiquote.org/wiki/Thomas_Edison; originally from a spoken statement uttered around 1903; it was later published in *Harper's Monthly* (September 1932)

vi http://en.wikiquote.org/wiki/Thomas_Edison; as quoted in an ad for GPU Nuclear Corporation, in *Black Enterprise* Vol. 16, No. 11 (June 1986), p. 79. Edison commented that —many of life's failures are people who did not realize how close they were to success when they gave up (this is presented as a statement of 1877, as quoted in *From Telegraph to Light Bulb with Thomas Edison* (2007) by Deborah Hedstrom, p. 22).

[vii] http://en.wikiquote.org/wiki/Thomas_Jefferson; Letter to John Adams (10 June 1815)

[viii] See http://www.statisticbrain.com/fear-of-public-speaking-statistics/

[ix] John M. Butler, "The 'Author' and the 'Finisher' of the Book of Mormon" *The Book of Mormon: Fourth Nephi Through Moroni, From Zion to Destruction* (1995) Religious Studies Center: BYU, pp. 61-68.

[x] John M. Butler, "A Few Thoughts of a Believing DNA Scientist" *Journal of Book of Mormon Studies* (2003) 12: 36-37.

[xi] Thought shared with the author from his father Doug Butler in August 2013.

[xii] See http://www.brainyquote.com/quotes/quotes/d/dalecarneg132157.html.

[xiii] 3 Nephi 27:29

Be Up and Doing

Learn. Act. Share. → Become!

Made in the USA
Middletown, DE
09 August 2021